SO YOU'VE BEEN APPOINTED EXECUTOR

SO YOU'VE BEEN APPOINTED EXECUTOR

Tom Carter, BA, MA, LLB

Self-Counsel Press
(a division of)
International Self-Counsel Press Ltd.
Canada   USA

Self-Counsel Press acknowledges the financial support of the Government of Canada through the Book Publishing Industry Development Program (BPIDP) for our publishing activities.

Printed in Canada.

First edition: 2002; Reprinted: 2003, 2004, 2005, 2006
Second edition: 2008

Library and Archives Canada Cataloguing in Publication

Carter, Tom (G. Thomas), 1950-
    So you've been appointed executor/Tom Carter. — 2nd ed.

ISBN: 978-1-55180-814-7

1. Executors and administrators—Canada—Popular works. I. Title.
KE831.Z82C37 2008   346.7105'6   C2007-906416-7   KF778.C37 2008

Material on pages 78, 79, 80, 81, and 87 is from Canada Revenue Agency and is reproduced with permission of the Minister of Public Works and Government Services Canada, 2006.

ANCIENT FOREST FRIENDLY Self-Counsel Press is committed to protecting the environment and to the responsible use of natural resources. We are acting on this commitment by working with suppliers and printers to phase out our use of paper produced from ancient forests. This book is one step toward that goal. It is printed on 100 percent ancient-forest-free paper (30 percent post-consumer recycled), processed chlorine- and acid-free.

Self-Counsel Press
(a division of)
International Self-Counsel Press Ltd.

1481 Charlotte Road   1704 North State Street
North Vancouver, BC V7J 1H1   Bellingham, WA 98225
Canada   USA

CONTENTS

INTRODUCTION

Each and every one of us has friends, family, or loved ones and even though we don't like it, the fact is that they — and we ourselves — are getting older every day. It goes without saying that we will all die eventually, and when we do, our debts and assets will have to be properly tended. That means each of us has to know something about what it means to be an executor so we will know what to do when the time comes.

There is another reason why we need to know something about what it means to be an executor. We all know that we should do our own wills, and if we know what being an executor is all about, we will be able to choose the right person, for the right reasons, to do the job in our own estates.

I wrote this book to explain to you what you need to know when you are an executor, and to help you choose the best executor for your own estate. If you decide you need help, I hope that the information I give about the various experts and resources available will help you get that help, at a reasonable cost. Finally, I hope it will help you avoid some agony when you are faced with one of the toughest decisions when you make your own will — who to name as your executor.

Throughout the book you will find tables of useful information and sample forms. Please note, each province and territory has its own forms for probate applications. To provide examples of each approved form for each jurisdiction would take two or three books the size of this one. Instead, in order to give you an idea of what those forms look like and what they say, I created my own generic sample forms that contain the basic information that is required everywhere. If you are looking after an estate yourself, you will have to get the correct forms for your province or territory.

Please note, this book is not intended to give you detailed information on each and every challenge that can arise in the course of looking after an estate; it's not an encyclopedia of the law of executorship. Nor does it try to give you precise technical details about the forms and requirements of each province and territory. It is not a comparative law treatise. If you have questions about the laws or procedures in your province or territory, you should consult a lawyer, accountant, or other estate professional in your area.

What this book does give you is an introduction to the predictable and unavoidable issues that each and every executor will face regardless of the size of the estate involved. These are the issues that my clients dealt with over and over again during my 20 years in private practice as augmented by the invaluable experience I gained during my two years as a trust officer with a major trust company.

Being an executor is a fascinating experience. Sometimes it is a short and simple task that only takes a little common sense. More often, however, it is a long and tiring experience that leads you into a tangle of legal jargon and principles that is overgrown with the unrealistic expectations of beneficiaries and the deep, sometimes unsettling, emotions that affect all of us when a loved one dies.

The purpose of this book, then, is to give you a general idea of what you need to know to get through that tangled thicket called being an executor. I hope it gives you the knowledge and confidence you need to make that journey successfully. Also, if you decide that you need professional help, I hope this book helps you find it.

When you get right down to it, I am talking about two priceless gifts that are merely the flip sides of what being an executor is all about — honouring the wishes of a deceased as quickly and inexpensively as possible and providing peace of mind for your loved ones and yourself in your will. When you think about it, it is within the power of each of us to give these gifts to those we love. I hope this book helps you do that.

Thank you for choosing this book, and good luck.

Part I
TO BE, OR NOT TO BE, AN EXECUTOR

1
FINDING OR CHOOSING AN EXECUTOR

1. It's Tough to Choose a Good Executor

When I was in law practice, I did a lot of work with people who were in agony. They were trying to make their wills, and they couldn't decide what to put in them. Whether the person making the will was single or married, had children or not, there were so many difficulties to work through. For some, the most painful decision was who to choose as beneficiaries and what to give them. Others, however, felt a more exquisite pain. They were struggling to choose the right executor — someone they could trust, absolutely and unconditionally, to carry out their wishes after they were gone.

As I worked with these people I discovered that they often had strong, preconceived ideas about how to choose an executor. People with families often didn't want to hurt anyone's feelings; they wanted to name everyone as executor so no one would feel left out. Others assumed that it was right to always name the eldest child, regardless of that child's ability to do the job. Those without family worried about burdening their friends with the job; they often were interested in hiring a professional person to do the job, but they were anxious about the extra cost that might involve, and about the possibility of delay in getting things done.

Sometimes the struggle to choose the right executor was so difficult that people were brought to a standstill and the will never did get done.

2. It's Tough to Be an Executor

I also worked with many executors, those who had been named in a will and were now called on to step in after the person died. These executors knew it was an important job but they were usually in the dark about what they were supposed to do and when they were supposed to do it. Some of them didn't even know they had been selected as executor until after the person died and the will came out of a lawyer's file or a safety deposit box. They had no chance to prepare themselves for this unique and demanding job.

Another thing I discovered was that most people who are named as executor don't like it. They found the experience to be much more difficult and time consuming than they expected. As the days and weeks wore on, any honour that might have been attached to the appointment faded. They often wished that the dearly departed had never thought of them at all. That impression was confirmed by a us survey I once saw that asked people who had been executors of an estate if they would like to do it again. The overwhelming majority said no.

I must admit, however, that I was not terribly empathetic to the plight of my executor clients. When I helped them look after an estate my job was relatively easy. I did the legal paperwork from the comfort of my desk while the executor handled everything else — making funeral arrangements, sorting through papers, disposing of foodstuffs and other perishable items, deciding what clothes to sell and what to send to charity, holding a garage sale for unwanted furniture or sending it to auction, tracking down bank accounts and other valuable assets, cancelling utility accounts, paying outstanding bills, claiming government and insurance benefits, getting a house or condo cleaned up and ready for sale, finding and working with a real estate agent and more.

3. How I Discovered What Being an Executor Was All About

I discovered that I really didn't know anything about the physical side of being an executor until I left law to become a trust officer with a trust company. Trust companies, as you will see, are often appointed executor in the wills of people who have no one else to choose and trust officers are the ones who do the executor work for the trust company. So it wasn't long after I joined the trust company that I got my first executor assignment and a first-hand taste of what being an executor was really all about. For obvious reasons of privacy, I can't tell you anything about the actual cases I worked on, but here is a typical, fictional case to illustrate. It's about Fred.

At the trust company, the first thing we did every morning was check the obituaries in the local newspaper. Then we checked those names against our records to see if we had a will for any of those people in our storage vault. On this particular day, we did. Fred had died, and because he had appointed the trust company his executor, we had his will in our storage vault.

The will was about 15 years old. It left everything in trust to Fred's only son, who lived hundreds of miles away. Unfortunately, the rest of the information in the file was sketchy. We could see that he was divorced, lived in a small condo in an unassuming part of town and had a small bank account with the trust company. Other than that, there was no information about assets, and we wondered why Fred had appointed us at all. Trust companies charge significant fees for the executor work they do so they are usually appointed only when the estate is large enough to justify those fees, and there was nothing in the file to suggest that Fred's estate was large.

We called the funeral home that had placed the obituary and discovered that the son was in town handling the arrangements. He was staying in a hotel, and he was desperately looking for his dad's will. We got in touch with the son and arranged a meeting at the funeral home. He came in looking confused, upset, and embarrassed. As he spoke we learned why. He and his father had been on very bad terms and hadn't seen each other, or even spoken to each other, for many years. He had never visited the condo and wasn't sure in which part of town it was located. He didn't even know that his dad had been ill. He had received a call from the hospital the day his father was admitted, and even though he had caught the next flight, by the time his taxi reached the hospital door Fred was dead.

The son said he was prepared to cover the cost of the funeral if necessary, but we were able to assure him that there was enough money in Fred's bank account for that. He was further relieved to learn that we had the will, and he was as puzzled as we were about the trust — he had no better idea of his dad's financial situation than we did. At that point, the funeral director produced a key that he had taken from Fred's pocket. Assuming it to be for the condo, we set off to take a look.

The condo was a modest two bedroom in an undistinguished part of the city. Being the home of a single, ailing man, it had a lived-in look. From speaking with neighbours, we discovered that Fred was a loner and his only social activity was going to bingo at the hall nearby. The son said that he was overwhelmed and didn't know where to start. He also said he had pressing business engagements back home and would be leaving right after the funeral. We told him that as executor, we would look after everything, and that our fees could be paid out of the sale of the condo. He agreed and a few days after the funeral we put on the rubber gloves and set to work.

By the time we were done we had discovered assets totalling a million dollars. Fred had investments with a variety of other financial institutions that had done very well. It was now obvious why Fred had appointed a trust company as his executor, and we were happy to carry on with our responsibilities. We reported to the son, who was as astonished as we were, and who was happy that we were there to look after everything for him.

4. The Need Will Never Go Away

Being an executor is a difficult, complex job. It requires knowledge of the law of wills, estates, and tax; comfort with a large amount of paperwork; willingness to work with various bureaucracies; familiarity with banking and insurance; excellent conflict-resolution skills; a lot of hard physical work; and the wisdom to recognize not only when you need help but also where to go to get it. Many of us hope it is a job that we will never have to do.

Unfortunately, as difficult or upsetting as the job of executor may be, the need for executors will never go away, because loved ones die. And as the population of this country gets older and passes on, two things are sure to happen — more of us will make our wills and more of us will discover that we have been named executor of the estate in a friend or family member's will.

5. Who This Book Is For

In Canada, the law of wills and estates is a provincial responsibility, which means that each province or territory sets its own rules and regulations for executors. A book of this size can't begin to provide specific details of procedures, requirements, and forms for each province or territory. However, even though those rules and regulations are not identical across the country, and the precise number and nature of tasks that have to be done vary according to the size and complexity of the estate, the basic idea is the same.

If you are mourning the death of a loved one who chose you as his or her executor, if you are trying to choose someone to be your executor in your will, or if you just want to inform yourself for that day in the future when you wake up and discover you are now an executor, read on. You'll learn what you must do, what pitfalls you can avoid, when you should consider getting help and how to find it.

2
THE FAQS OF LIFE FOR EXECUTORS

One morning the phone rings just as you are struggling to get out the door. You throw down your briefcase, run back to the kitchen, pick up the phone, and freeze. It's terrible news. A voice tells you that your brother, mother, aunt, grandfather, or friend is dead. As you try to comprehend this, the voice goes on to tell you something else. It says that you are the executor of the will.

As if the grief over losing a loved one isn't enough, you are flooded with an entirely different set of anxieties as a whole set of questions run through your head: What is an executor? What does an executor do? How did I get that job? Do I have to do it?

This chapter will give you a general idea of the facts of life for executors by answering the most frequently asked questions. Let's start by looking at what an executor is, and how you got this challenging and interesting job.

1. What Is an Executor?

In simplest terms, an executor is the person named in a will to look after things when the person who made the will dies. In other words, the deceased decided a certan individual was best for the job, and said so in his or her will. So when someone dies the answer to "Who is the executor of this estate?" is found by looking at the will. This information is easy to find: the clause naming the executor is usually the first or second item in a will.

2. What Are Sole, Joint, and Alternate Executors?

If the will names only one executor, he or she is called a *sole executor*. Often, however, a will names more than one executor, and they are called *joint executors*.

A sole executor acts alone. Joint executors, however, must act in harmony, which means they must agree on each and every decision. This can be difficult, and when they fail to agree, they have to go to court to get a judge's ruling to break the logjam. That is something to be avoided, of course, because of the expense and delay involved, so a well-drafted will should contain a clause that avoids the problem. Sometimes these clauses say that the majority rules, sometimes they give decision making power to one executor while directing him or her to consult with the others at all times. I've even seen clauses that direct executors to go to a mediator if they cannot agree.

There is another category of executor that must be mentioned. It is possible that one or more of the named executors may not be available to do the job when the time comes. There are a number of logical reasons for this: the executor may have died before the person who made the will died, the executor may be unable to do the job because of illness or incapacity, he or she may be to busy or may feel that the job is too difficult, or the executor may have moved away. To cover these possibilities, most people name a backup executor in the will. These backups are called *alternate executors*, and they have power only if the named executor is unable or unwilling to act.

3. To Whom Am I Responsible As Executor?

An executor must always act with the interests of many people in mind. These people are the *beneficiaries*, those who are entitled to receive some or all of the assets of the deceased according to the will, and the *creditors of the estate*, those to whom the deceased owes money. We will talk more about specific responsibilities to these people in Chapter 7.

4. The Will Says I'm Executor, So I Am, Right?

People assume that because they have seen a will signed by the deceased and it names them as executor, they can assume it means what it says. However, an important legal principle must be kept in mind before jumping to that conclusion. It's called *testamentary freedom*, and it says that anyone is free to make a new will anytime they wish as long as they have the necessary mental capacity to do so. This means that you must be sure you are looking at the very last will of the deceased before you can say with certainty that you are the executor of that person's estate.

You may think this is an unlikely problem. You know how much trouble and effort it took to get your own will done, and you can't imagine people going through that more than necessary, so you are tempted to think that the chances of this not being the last will are slim. However, while lawyers lament the fact that many people never manage to get one will done, let alone several, there are people who change their wills regularly. One famous person who did that was Hollywood producer, inventor, pilot, millionaire, and recluse Howard Hughes. When he died several years ago, he left a large number of wills behind, each leaving his estate to different people. This issue was not so much who was the real executor as it was who was to get his vast estate, but the lawsuit to decide which will was his true last will dragged on for years, and while it did, everyone and everything was in a state of uncertainty.

So you can't assume you are the true executor until you are certain that you have the true last will of the person who died. But how can you be sure? You might feel confident if you got the will from a lawyer's office. Most lawyers store their clients' wills in their office vaults, and you might think, "If the lawyer doesn't know if this is the last will, who does?" So you check with the lawyer, who assures you that there aren't any other wills on file for that person.

But that isn't a complete assurance for a number of reasons, as the lawyer will quickly point out. First, people change lawyers, and some people will go to another lawyer to make another will without telling the first one. Second, people move, and they often do a new will in their new community with a new lawyer. Third, people can make a will on their own using a will kit or, in the places where handwritten wills (called *holograph wills*) are legal, they can simply write their own will by hand. So lawyers do not always know when clients have done new wills, and every lawyer has a vault containing old wills that are no longer valid. They gather dust, and all the lawyer can say is they are the last wills the lawyer did for that person.

If lawyers can't be sure, who can? It would be nice if there was a central place you could go to see if the will you have is the last one, such as a government office or a website listing all the wills ever made, but unfortunately there are no such places. None of the provinces or territories operate a centralized will registry system. Even if they did, how would you force people to use it? You would have to make sure that people knew about it, and even if they did, there would always be those who would object to using it. They will not want to put information about something as personal as a will in a place that is accessible to other people. Then there are those who might like the idea but never get around to using it because they are too busy or the system is inconvenient.

Private companies try to start will registries from time to time. The latest I am aware of is an Internet-based system offered by a group in Calgary. The idea is that when you make your will, you send information about where it is kept to the registry and pay a one-time fee. They enter the information in their system and when you die, your family or friends can search the system and find out where to look for your will. This could be useful for finding a will but it still offers no reassurance that you have the true last will. In Chapter 6, I will talk more about the process of searching for the last will of a deceased. For now, keep in mind that you can't be sure you are the executor until you are sure you have the very last will of the deceased in your hands. The only way to be absolutely sure of that is to have that will probated by the appropriate court, usually called the surrogate court.

5. What's Probate, and Why Do I Need It?

The word *probate* comes from the Latin word meaning proof. *Probating a will* means proving to the surrogate court that the will you have is in fact the very last will of the deceased. The process is called *making an application for probate*, and the procedure that must be followed is found in the set of rules that govern the operation of the court. In the case of a surrogate court, these are called the *surrogate rules* or the *probate rules*.

The technicalities of an application for probate are beyond the scope of this book. For our purposes it is enough to say that if your probate application is in order — if you have provided all the necessary information, notified all the necessary people, and if you have provided satisfactory proof that the will is the last will of the deceased — and if the judge accepts it, then he or she will order the clerk of the court to issue formal papers. Usually called a *probate certificate*, these papers tell the world that as far as the court is concerned this is the last will of the deceased. That means the appointment of the executor is confirmed and it is safe for everyone to do what the will says. This is a huge advantage and lets the executor get on with the job without any worries.

A second advantage of probate is that it gives the executor legal protection that he or she would not otherwise have. For example, the surrogate rules tell the executor what he or she has to do to notify beneficiaries — both named and unnamed — of their interest in the will. It is easy to identify the named beneficiaries because they are named in the will, but there are others who are not named who still might have a right to share the estate assets. An obvious example would be family members who were left out of the will for some reason, either a spouse or a child under the age of majority or one who is over majority age but cannot earn a living due to a physical or mental disability.

The rules also tell the executor how to notify *creditors*, those who might be owed money by the deceased. Typically, the executor is allowed to run a notice in the newspaper telling creditors that if they don't provide proof of their claim within a fixed time, they will be barred from making a claim later. If a claim is not made, the executor can safely ignore it.

A third advantage of probate is the protection it gives executors from complaints by beneficiaries or creditors that he or she did not handle the estate properly. An executor can have his records and accounts reviewed and approved by a surrogate judge at any time. Anyone who has a complaint has the right to be heard. Once the judge is satisfied that everything has been done correctly, the court will issue an order approving the executor's accounts, and the executor is free from further complaints.

Note that the executor is not the only one who takes comfort in the security offered by a probate certificate. Financial institutions like banks, investment brokers, and insurance companies usually require probate before they feel safe handing over money and other assets of the deceased to the executor, and government land title offices will usually not let the executor make ownership changes to the deceased's lands without one.

I will have more to say about probate, and whether or not it necessary or prudent to get a probate certificate in Chapter 6.

6. When Does My Authority As Executor Begin?

Another important legal principle of which an executor must be aware is this: *a will speaks from the moment of death*. This is important for two reasons. First, it means that regardless of when a will is signed, it doesn't have any force or effect until the person who made it dies. For example, someone might sign a will in 1970 and never do another one. If that person died in 2000, the 1970 will is still valid, but it would deal with the person's estate as it is at death not as it was in 1970.

Second, it means that even though you were named executor in 1970, you will have no power and no responsibility to do anything with that person's estate until the moment of his or her death 30 years later. This may seem obvious but in reality it is commonly misunderstood. People who make wills are called *testators*, and they and their executors often assume that the executor has the right to take charge of the testator's affairs while the testator is still alive. They think that if the testator becomes incapacitated due to illness or injury, the executor can step in, take charge of the testator's accounts, pay his or her bills and look after all things financial. This is simply not true. As we have just seen, a will speaks from death and an executor's authority does too.

The problem is that people often confuse a will with another document called an *enduring power of attorney*. If a testator wants to give his or her executor the power to step in and manage things before the testator dies as a result of a stroke or any other incapacitating event, then he or she has to prepare an enduring power of attorney saying so. Discussion of enduring powers of attorney are beyond the scope of this book, but you can find more information about them in my second book, for Self-Counsel Press, *Write Your Legal Will in 3 Easy Steps*.

Incidentally, it's important to know that being named an executor in a will is not the only way you can become responsible for looking after the estate of a deceased person. You can be appointed as administrator of the estate in a court order, and as administrator, you receive the same powers and responsibilities as an executor. This happens when the deceased person didn't leave a will, when the will didn't name an executor, or when the executor and any alternates named in the will refuse the job. In all these cases the law allows those who have an interest in seeing that the estate gets handled properly — typically close relatives of the deceased or beneficiaries named in the will — to ask the court to be appointed as administrators.

In recognition of the fact that both executors and administrators look after estates, some provinces have adopted the term *personal representative* to describe both. In this book, however, I will stick with the familiar and widely recognized term *executor*. The powers and responsibilities of executors and administrators are virtually identical, but there is one big difference which relates to when those powers begin. The law says that the powers of an executor begin at the moment of death, but the powers of an administrator don't begin until a surrogate judge signs a court order appointing the administrator. However, this is often a distinction without a difference. In practical terms the only thing an executor can safely do without a probate certificate is make funeral arrangements for the deceased and arrange payment of the funeral home's bill.

In simplest terms, you are an executor because the deceased named you as such in his or her will. As we will see, being an executor means being a legal expert, an accountant, a bureaucrat, a banker, an investment advisor, a mediator, a psychologist, a communicator, and a tax authority all in one. Being an executor combines all these jobs, and to make it worse, it's a job that is done in the toughest of times — right after the death of a loved one. No wonder it is a job that people like to avoid. Eventually, however many of us will find ourselves called on to do it. When we are, we should keep in mind the basics:

- An executor is the person so named in the last will of the deceased

- An executor's authority begins only when the person who wrote he will dies

7. What Do I Have to Do As Executor?

As I said in Chapter 1, the job of executor is a complex one that involves a hundred or more different tasks depending on the size and complexity of the estate. Fortunately, these tasks can be organized under eight principle headings. The eight duties of an executor are:

- Make reasonable funeral arrangements

- Find and take control of the assets of the deceased

- Prepare an inventory, value the assets, and keep an account

- Find and probate the will, if necessary

- Deal with debts and claims against the estate

- Pay any taxes owing by the deceased and the estate

- Account to, and get releases from, the beneficiaries

- Distribute to the beneficiaries

It looks simple enough, doesn't it? But as I said earlier, surveys tell us that many people who have done it once don't want to do it again. That's because they learned the hard way that being an executor can be a long and arduous task. They simply weren't prepared for the job before they began and perhaps they did not know that they had a choice — just because they were named executor in the will didn't mean they had to take it on. I discuss what to do if you don't want the job later, but before deciding that you need to know what the risks are.

8. What Liabilities Do I Face As Executor?

Law books use a colourful Latin word, *devastavit*, to describe an executor's liability. It suggests the image of someone deliberately destroying estate assets. Another graphic word that lawyers sometimes use is *waste*, which always made me think of estate property being casually tossed into the garbage bin, or left to rot.

These vivid words are appropriate. They remind us that your number-one task as executor is to make sure that the assets of the estate are properly cared for. If they are not — if they are destroyed, lost, or devalued because of your neglect — you will be personally responsible to make up any loss.

Aside from not looking after estate assets properly, you can also be liable for failing to carry out your duties properly. It is impossible to make a complete list of such failures, but the most common of them are listed here. As you can see, each one is the reverse of one of the executor's duties I listed earlier:

- Paying unreasonable funeral expenses
- Failure to search for and find all the estate assets
- Failure to protect and manage the estate's assets
- Failure to find and pay all legally payable debts or paying debts that are not legally payable
- Failure to file all necessary tax returns and pay all taxes
- Failure to invest the estate assets properly while looking after the estate
- Failure to identify all beneficiaries
- Failure to pay all appropriate beneficiaries
- Failure to properly account for the handling of the estate assets

If you are guilty of one of these failures, you will also be personally liable for the loss, which means you will have to pay for it, perhaps with interest, out of your own pocket. That's why being an executor is a serious business, and why it is important to be aware of some of these pitfalls into which an unwary or inexperienced executor could fall. Since these are the flip-side of the executor's duties, the next eight chapters take a closer look at what those duties involve.

9. What Are the Attributes of a Good Executor?

We are not far into the book, but you are probably already asking, "Why me?" Why did the deceased pick you? Good question. Ideally, you were chosen because you are the right person for the job. You possess all the attributes of a good executor, such as patience, wisdom, knowledge, discretion, and you have the time required to do what has to be done.

Unfortunately, when I was in law practice I saw many people choose executors for other reasons. Some felt it was always necessary to choose the eldest child, preferably a son, regardless of his character and abilities. Others felt they had to be fair, and they would insist on naming all their children, even when there were serious doubts about the ability of those children to get along and get the job done.

Not only did people pick executors for such reasons, but many also never told their executors that they had been picked for the job at all. The executor wouldn't know anything about it until the death, when, to his or her total surprise, he or she would find out that they had been named to do this important task. Some would accept the responsibility and carry on, but others just wanted to know how to get out of it.

10. What If I Don't Want to Be Executor?

Fortunately, an executor who is not able or willing to do the job has an option: he or she can refuse to act. This is called *renouncing*, and it is done by signing a form called a *renunciation*. The precise form you need is found in the surrogate rules of your province, and once it is signed, the job passes to the alternate executor named in the will, if there is one. If no alternate is named in the will, then someone has to make an application to the local surrogate court to be appointed administrator of the estate, as we discussed earlier.

11. How Do I Decide to Be an Executor or Not?

Here are some questions to ask yourself as you think about whether or not you want to act as executor:

- **How complex is the will?** Does it set up trusts that you will have to look after for years and years? Does it put conditions on gifts that you will have to interpret and enforce? Does it make gifts to people who are now dead without any alternative gifts? Does it contain unusual clauses or stipulations like a gift to a beneficiary for his or her life and then the leftovers go to someone else when that beneficiary dies (called a *life estate with a gift over*)?

- **How complex is the estate?** Is it cash, a house, and some ordinary investments with which you are familiar or does it contain businesses, partnerships, rental properties, foreign assets, exotic investments or anything else unfamiliar to you?

- **Do you have the time, energy, and knowledge to do the job properly?** This is the age of burnout and stress. Do you work very long hours? Are you caught in the caregiver's sandwich — looking after kids while also looking after aging parents or even grandparents? Are you volunteering until you can't volunteer anymore?

- **Do you have a conflict of interest?** For example, are you both beneficiary and executor, and there is some dispute about the validity of the gift to you?

- **Are the beneficiaries in harmony?** Even the simplest, most straightforward will becomes a nightmare to look after if the beneficiaries are unhappy, and take steps to have the will declared invalid because they think it was not properly signed, or the deceased was pressured into signing it, or the deceased didn't have full mental capacity when it was signed. Even if the will is valid, they can still make life miserable for an executor if they are disappointed with the gifts they are given. Many executors tell stories about the horrible fights over the one-of-a-kind family heirlooms such as a set of rare china, the family Bible, or grandpa's war medals. Are you up for the strain?

- **Is the estate insolvent?** This happens when there is not enough in the estate to pay all the deceased's debts, let alone enough to fulfil the gifts to the beneficiaries. There are also estates in which there is enough to pay the debts but not enough to pay each beneficiary in full. Then complicated rules about proportioning the gifts apply.

- **Is there a problem finding the will?** You think you are executor because the deceased said you were, but you have only a photocopy of the will, or you may have no copy at all. What if you don't find the original? Then what? Do you have the time and energy to find out?

- **Are there any lawsuits pending?** Was the deceased being sued for any reason before death? Was he or she involved in a nasty divorce that hadn't been settled before death? Was the death due to an accident caused by the deceased, and will there be a lawsuit against the estate over that? Was the accident caused by someone else, and will the estate be starting a lawsuit to recover compensation?

- **Will there be tax problems?** Did the deceased file and pay taxes every year or is he or she in arrears? For how long? Are there capital gain issues to sort out? Do you understand the tax treatment of rrsps, life insurance, investments, land, and other assets? Do you want to learn? Are you comfortable knowing that if you don't file all necessary returns and pay all taxes owing, you might be liable to pay them yourself?

- **Do you have the expertise?** Do you know enough to do it all? If not, are you comfortable seeking out and working with qualified professionals?

12. Can I Change My Mind after I Start?

Just as you do not have to act as executor if you don't want to, you do have some freedom to change your mind and back out after you start, but there is one important difference. The executor who decides not to act before doing anything with the estate is free of any liability, but the executor who starts the job and then backs out is not. He or she will be liable for any losses that occur during that time.

The law calls this *intermeddling*, and it applies when —

- you take control of estate assets and do with them what an executor would do, and

- other people are led to believe by your actions that you are the executor and they rely on that.

If you don't want to act as executor, you must be very careful that you don't do anything that makes it look like you are the executor. This may seem harsh but it makes sense. If you do something that causes a loss, the concept of intermeddling means that those who are supposed to benefit from the estate get the same degree of protection whether you are officially the executor or not. It also shows that there is an element of acceptance involved in being appointed executor: if you signal your acceptance of the job by doing something significant to the estate, you become liable.

Two actions that amount to intermeddling are taking possession of assets owned by the deceased or advising someone in writing that you are executor so they rely on this and act accordingly. However, making enquiries about the assets and debts of the deceased without taking control of them or arranging payment of reasonable funeral costs does not amount to intermeddling.

Intermeddling is a complicated legal concept. If you have concerns about it, you should check with a lawyer.

13. Can I Get Help?

If the answers to the questions above make you uncomfortable you will be relieved to know that you can always get help. Some wills make this explicit. They contain a clause that says the executor has the power to hire agents to help him or her with the work. Even if the will doesn't have that clause, the law is clear. You can still hire help, but if you do hire help, you still have a duty to act — you must make all the major decisions. You can't delegate decision-making power to someone else. That means the experts you hire will advise you, then you make the decisions based on their advice. However, you don't have to carry out the detailed work yourself. The experts can do that, but only after they get your instructions.

14. Who Can Help Me and How Do I Find Them?

The executor-assistance industry is dominated by three traditional players: lawyers, accountants, and trust companies. The big three offer the most comprehensive services, but there is a new group that is challenging them: the paralegal services. There are also the services for specific parts of the estate, which includes tax preparers, real estate agents, and personal-property appraisers. Let's look at the advantages and disadvantages of each, and how to find the right one, or ones, for your estate.

15. Lawyers

The litany of complaints and anxieties about lawyers is depressingly familiar. It includes statements like these: lawyers charge too much, lawyers give you no say in what is done, lawyers are too slow, lawyers don't keep you informed, lawyers charge for every phone call, postage stamp, and photocopy: the list goes on.

15.1 Advantages of using lawyers

Nonetheless, the first person an executor thinks of turning to for help is a lawyer, and there are many good reasons for that. One is that an experienced estate lawyer can look after every aspect of an estate. Some lawyers will do everything, including estate accounts and tax returns. Others don't, but anything they don't do they refer to the appropriate professional — someone with whom the lawyer has worked before who often charges a reduced fee in return for the business.

Another advantage is that a good estate lawyer can usually get everything done faster than you can. This may be hard to believe. People think lawyers stretch things out, especially those who charge by the hour, and though there may be some who do that, most lawyers are just as eager as you are to finish an estate file because normally that's when they get paid.

Finally, when you use a lawyer you get the benefit of his or her malpractice insurance. No one deliberately hires a lawyer who is going to make a mistake, but once in a while mistakes happen. If you are looking after the estate yourself and you make a mistake, you and your personal assets are on the line, but if the lawyer makes a mistake, his or her insurance company should pick up the loss.

15.2 Lawyers' fees

Of course, it costs money to hire a lawyer, and estate lawyers are no exception. Lawyers' fees for estate work are usually based on the value of the estate multiplied by a percentage taken from a tariff set by the provincial government, by the local surrogate court, or by the local lawyers' organization. However, lawyers like estate files because they offer comfortable fees for fairly routine work. That means there is competition for estate files, and competition means you can usually negotiate a fee that is less than the recommended tariff in your area. This is especially true if the estate is not complicated. To cover themselves, most lawyers will reserve the right to charge more if an unexpected problem arises once they start work.

In the past, lawyers worked on an all or nothing basis; they insisted on doing everything that needed to be done on a file or nothing at all. They did not allow clients who wanted to save money and who were capable of doing some of the things that needed doing to do them. That's because lawyers said that if they were taking the risk that goes along with managing any legal problem, they wanted to make sure they were in control. If a mistake was made, at least it would be made by them. Estates have always been an exception to this because there is a lot of running around and information gathering to be done, and lawyers have been happy to leave most of that to the executor. Because of this, and because most estate files are fairly predictable, lawyers usually set a fixed fee for their services.

In some cases, a lawyer may take on an estate file on an hourly rate basis, especially where the facts and details are not known and it is impossible to say for sure what has to be done. Of course, if there is a lawsuit involving the estate, fees will be charged on an hourly basis. Regardless of how fees are set, the executor has an absolute right to know what they are and how they will be calculated before the lawyer starts work.

15.3 Finding a good estate lawyer

Some lawyers know more about estate work than others. Don't assume that the person who did your divorce or your house purchase is the best person to help you with an estate. Nor should you be overly swayed by fancy ads in the yellow pages or on television; any lawyer can buy those. The fact is, that even in this media-happy world, lawyers still get most of their work from referrals, so when you are looking for a lawyer you need to learn how to make the referral network work for you. Even if you have never had the pleasure of darkening the door of a law office yourself, your friends, neighbours, and acquaintances have, and they will be happy to tell you if the lawyer they saw was worth seeing again or not.

To find the best lawyer to help you, follow the three steps outlined below.

15.3a Step 1: Get the names of five good lawyers

Make a list of everyone you can think of who might have used a lawyer. Include people from these categories and any others you can think of:

- Work
- Church/synagogue/mosque
- Parents or teachers at your children's school
- Community organizations
- Night school classmates
- Golf/curling/tennis...
- Neighbours
- Mechanic
- Doctor or nurse

- Barber/hairdresser
- Insurance agent
- Banker/financial planner
- People you volunteer with
- Landlord

Talk to these people and get the names, phone numbers, and addresses of as many lawyers as you can. Select three to five of them for whatever reason you want — a very strong recommendation, the office is close to where you live, you like the idea of having a woman lawyer, whatever. Call this your short list and move to Step 2.

15.3b Step 2: Work the phone

Call each of the lawyers on your short list. If you get through to the lawyer right away, that's great. If you don't, don't worry about it; it doesn't mean the lawyer doesn't want to talk to you. Everyone is using voice mail to manage their calls these days, and those that don't still have receptionists. Say you are the executor of an estate and you are looking for a good estate lawyer to help you. Leave your name and number and when you are available for a return call.

When the lawyer calls back, do some quick weeding by asking these short questions:

- Do you do estate work?
- A lot or a little?
- How do you stay up to date with estate law?
- How do you charge?
- Is the first visit free?

The answers will tell you a lot about whether or not the lawyer is looking for, and is qualified to do, estate work. You want to hear answers like these:

- "Yes, I do estate work."
- "Lots of it. It's almost all I do."
- "I go to monthly estate discussion groups, belong to several estate law organizations, go to every estate law seminar, and teach the estate law portion of the bar admission course."

- "That depends on the estate."
- "It sure is."

If you like what you hear, make an appointment and move to Step 3.

15.3c Step 3: Visit the prospects

First impressions are crucial. From them you can learn a lot about how the lawyer values you and your work. When you show up for the appointment, pay attention to the condition of the office. Is the waiting area tidy? Does it contain reading material about wills and estates? How are you treated? How long is the wait?

When you get into the lawyer's office, what do you see? Desks and furniture littered with other people's confidential documents, or is everything orderly and kept away from unauthorized eyes?

When the interview begins, how does the lawyer treat you? Is the lawyer watching the clock or are you given the time you need to get the information you want? Does the lawyer encourage you to tell all your story or are you cut short by pre-packaged jargon and big words you don't understand? Are your questions answered to your satisfaction? Are fees mentioned right up front and is the basis for charging them clear?

After visiting three lawyers, you should have a pretty good idea if you want to work with any one of them. If not, go back to Step 1 and begin again.

16. Accountants

After lawyers, people probably think of accountants as the next source of help with estates. That's because accountants do taxes, and taxes are a big concern of executors. Lately, however, another reason accountants come to mind is they have been actively marketing themselves to people who need help managing and planning their finances as they get older. That puts accountants in line for the estate work after those people die. Chartered accountants in particular have identified this area as a specialty, and they are taking courses to learn how they can best meet the needs of this growing segment of our population.

16.1 Advantages of using accountants

Accountants will handle the tax returns and the accounting required in an estate, and what they can't do they farm out to other professionals, often for reduced fees. For example, legal work like getting probate of the will goes to lawyers who know estate law and who often charge less in return for the work.

Accountants also rely on executors to do the leg work and to bring in all the information they need, but otherwise they will not turn over any of the tax and accounting work to you once they have been hired for the job. If you think the tax returns and accounts for beneficiaries in your case are so simple you can do them yourself, either you don't need an accountant or you are misleading yourself. Why not take advantage of a free visit to talk to an accountant and find out? Like lawyers, most accountants offer an initial consultation for free.

Finally, accountants must also carry malpractice insurance, which covers them if they make a mistake.

16.2 Accountants' fees

Accountants usually charge on an hourly basis, though some may have set fees for routine estate work. Like other professionals, accountants expect you to ask about their fees before you hire them, so the best time to clear that up is before they get started.

16.3 Finding a good estate accountant

To find a good accountant who knows and likes estate work, follow the same three-step procedure as for lawyers, but change the questions from "estate law" to "estate accounting."

17. Trust Companies

The third member of the big three is the trust companies. Originally established to manage the affairs of the rich and famous, trust companies have evolved over the years into clones of normal banks but with better hours. In the past decade, with the repeal of government rules that prevented banks from owning trust companies, all the major trust companies are now owned by banks.

17.1 How trust companies become executors

In spite of the fact that trust companies now look like banks, they are still in the business of looking after estates. They get estate work in two ways: either they are named executor in a will, or they are hired by an executor who wants help looking after an estate, in which case they are called the agent of the executor. As agent, the trust company takes over the day-to-day handling of the estate and advises the executor when something complex comes up because, as we've seen, an executor can't turn over decision-making authority to anyone else.

17.2 When to consider a trust company

Trust companies are still primarily interested in the estates of the rich. They will not take on an estate unless it meets their minimum size. Some companies have a minimum of $1 million and others are higher, though some may still take estates as low as $500 000. So the first factor you have to consider is whether or not your estate is big enough for a trust company, and the only way to find out is to call and ask.

If your estate is big enough but simple (for example, the million dollars is all in a home, and the will tells you to sell that home and divide the money equally among the beneficiaries) you might not need a trust company to help you. However, there are other factors to consider. If there is a family feud or a lawsuit, or when the estate includes complex assets that require sophisticated management or that lead to challenging tax problems (such as land other than the deceased's house, a business, publicly traded shares, art collections, or assets in other countries) hiring a trust company might be a good choice.

17.3 Advantages of a trust company

One advantage of trust companies is that unlike lawyers and accountants they do take over the leg work. Their employees do everything, including searching and securing the residence, arranging sale of unwanted household goods, tracking down bank accounts, and so on. They also have staff who do the tax returns and accounts for the estate, so these tasks are not farmed out. However, they do farm out the legal work. Typically they hire the lawyer who made the will to get probate, but only if that lawyer gives them a substantial reduction of his or her fee. Also, trust companies are insured for any mistakes they might make.

17.4 Trust company fees and fee agreements

All this comes at a price, of course. Like all executors, trust companies must charge in accordance with the fee scale that is in force in the province where the estate is located. However since they are in the business of making a profit they always charge at the high end of those scales. Also, trust companies don't want to get into arguments with executors or beneficiaries about their fees so they always get a fee agreement signed before they start work. If the deceased appointed the trust company in the will, he or she likely signed a fee agreement when the will was signed. If not, and the executor is hiring the trust company, the executor signs it. Regardless of when it was signed, these fee agreements are legal in every province, although Manitoba requires that they be reviewed by a surrogate judge before the trust company pays itself.

17.5 Finding a good trust company

One way for an executor to find a trust company is to look them up in the yellow pages. Another way is to ask the staff at your bank branch if they have a trust department that offers estate services. Once you have a few leads, phone and ask if they handle estates of your size and if they do arrange a meeting with their local representatives. Don't be afraid to ask if they will meet you at your house or office if you prefer. Most of them will make house calls because competition for high value estates is fierce and they will do anything they can to get your business.

At the meeting, ask who will be doing the actual work. This is important because trust companies are no different from other companies: they spent much of the 1980s and 1990s downsizing staff and streamlining operations. As a result, very little of the work will be done in your local office. Instead your file will be sent to a central processing department hundreds or thousands of miles away from where you are. That means whenever you phone to ask a question, your local contact may not know what is going on and will have to send your request to the processing centre for a reply. Depending on conditions there, you may wait awhile to get an answer, and when it comes, it may be a vague statement that the file is in for processing and the papers should be available in a couple of weeks. This can be frustrating.

18. The Challengers: Paralegal Services

Paralegal services sprang up in the late 1980s and early 1990s. They were a response to the perception that lawyers' fees for less complicated legal problems like uncontested divorces, traffic tickets, and simple incorporations were getting too high for the average person. More recently, some paralegals have begun helping executors with simple estates.

18.1 Advantages and disadvantages of paralegals

As with everything in life, you get what you pay for. Paralegals may be cheaper than lawyers, but they are not regulated by the government and they do not carry the kind of malpractice insurance that lawyers do. Having said that, some of them have a great deal of estate experience: they may have worked for trust companies or as secretaries for estate lawyers. If you are thinking of using one, ask some very pointed questions about their estate experience with the following in mind.

18.1a Clarify what they will do

Be clear on exactly what they are going to do for you. Are they just getting probate or are they going to do the accounts and report to the beneficiaries? What happens if a problem comes up like a beneficiary who refuses to sign a release?

18.1b Keep control of the estate assets yourself

Never let the paralegal take possession or control of the estate assets. Since they are not insured like lawyers, all could be lost if the paralegal goes out of business before the job is finished. You could be left to cover the estate debts and gifts to beneficiaries out of your own pocket.

18.1c Be clear on fees

Make sure you know exactly what the fee will be and how it will be calculated before you agree to hire them. Don't be afraid to take their quote to a lawyer for comparison. Make sure that the paralegal is not offering less service for the same money.

18.1d Finding paralegals

The best way to find paralegals is probably through their ads in the newspaper or yellow pages, although I once saw a tear-off sheet on the bulletin board of a local supermarket. It had been placed there by a retired trust company employee who was looking for estate work to do from his home.

19. Specific Services

19.1 Tax-preparation services

The tax-preparation services that spring up in malls at tax-return time may also do estate returns. However, as you will see, the issues that come up in an estate may go far beyond the issues that apply to the average working person. If you have a very simple estate with no complex tax issues, they may be a good choice for you. Be sure to ask about fees before you hire them, and who pays if they make a mistake and the government assesses a late filing fee or a penalty.

Before using one of these services, consider taking their fee quote to an accountant for comparison. You may find that the accountant will match it or will point out a problem that you or the tax service overlooked.

19.2 Real estate agents

Real estate agents are always looking for estate properties to list and sell, and there are no unusual problems selling them except one: it takes so much longer to get all the paperwork done when an estate is the seller. Unfortunately, realtors often overlook that. They forget that the executor has no authority until he or she gets probate of the will, and they get the executor to sign a listing anyway. Then, when the place sells, they forget about probate again and don't leave enough time for it to issue. Buyers who expect keys on a certain day get very upset when they are told that they can't get in because probate isn't available yet. Keep this in mind when working with a realtor to sell an estate property. Make sure that the realtor knows that any offers he or she brings to you must allow enough time for you to get probate.

As far as I know, there aren't any realtors who specialize only in estate sales. To choose a good realtor, use your personal contacts to narrow the field then interview the prospects. Remember they are salespeople, and a big part of their success rides on selling themselves to you. Don't let yourself be pressured. There are lots of good realtors from whom to choose, and until you get probate, time is on your side.

19.3 Personal property appraisers, evaluation specialists, and auctioneers

I was once on television promoting my second book from Self-Counsel Press, *Wills Guide for Canada* (it is now called *Write Your Legal Will in 3 Easy Steps*). The show was about antiques, and the main guest was an appraiser of personal property who described himself as an evaluation specialist. He is one of those people who know everything about everything — jewellery, collectibles, furniture, glassware, you name it. The tv crew and other guests brought in treasured family objects, and he told them if these were valuable or not. To our surprise, many were.

During a break, I spoke to his assistant, who said that they were getting more and more calls from executors who had houses full of interesting pieces but they didn't know if these pieces were valuable. This man would go take a look and give the executors a report, but then the executor had another problem — how to sell the items for the best price?

Seeing a business opportunity, he began holding on-site sales for those executors, and he said it is one of the fastest growing parts of his business. It's like a giant garage sale but with one critical difference: you have an expert on site to make sure that anything that is truly valuable doesn't get sold for a couple of bucks.

If you need an evaluation and sale of personal property, check the yellow pages, watch your local consumer shows, or listen to talk radio to find out if anyone is offering this service in your area.

If all you want is an idea of the value of items, you can get that from a personal-property appraiser. They are usually listed in the yellow pages. Or if you just want someone to sell things, you can try an auctioneer. They will truck any saleable items to their warehouse to be sold with other material on the next scheduled sale day. Auctioneers are listed in the yellow pages as well.

I hope this chapter has answered most of your questions about what it means to be an executor. Now we are ready to look closely at the eight duties of an executor.

Part II
THE EIGHT DUTIES OF THE EXECUTOR

3
DUTY NUMBER 1:
MAKE REASONABLE
FUNERAL ARRANGEMENTS

Note: It is a good idea to acquire the deceased's death certificate, will and power of attorney documents (if available) before you proceed. Some institutions will not be able to help you unless you can prove you are the executor.

1. The Executor Makes Decisions about the Funeral

One day, when I was in law practice, I got a call from a funeral director. He had several members of a family in his office and they had been having a heated discussion about funeral arrangements for a deceased member of the family. Fortunately, there was a will and it named one of them as executor. The funeral director asked me who had the right to make final decisions about the funeral. I told him the executor did, and I imagined him holding out the phone so that everyone in the room could hear me say that. He thanked me, and since I never heard anything further from him, I presumed that the funeral went ahead without further arguments.

There are two key points to remember with regard to funeral expenses. First, as I told the funeral director (who probably knew it all along but who wanted the feuding family to hear it from an independent authority), the law gives the executor the right to make funeral arrangements; not the spouse, not the brothers and sisters, not anyone else related to or devoted to the deceased. In fact, not even the deceased gets the last word. The will may contain lengthy and elaborate instructions for a funeral, but the law says that the executor is not bound to follow them. That's because the wishes of the deceased may be quite unreasonable.

For example, a will might say that the deceased's body is to be transported to India to be cremated. Then his ashes are to be sprinkled over the Himalayan Mountains from a chartered aircraft carrying all his friends. An executor reading that in a will would blanch. Who knows if such a thing is even possible? What is the policy of the Indian government on allowing bodies into the country? Can outsiders be cremated there? Where? Does this conflict with any local religious or cultural values? How do you charter an aircraft, and what does the deceased mean by "his friends"? Who are they? How are they chosen?

2. The Costs Must Be Reasonable

Which brings us to the second point: the cost. The law says that funeral expenses must be reasonable given the size of the estate, and that applies no matter what the will says. That's because the law will not allow a modest estate to be squandered on lavish funeral arrangements, which might leave nothing for the deceased's creditors, not to mention his or her beneficiaries. So the executor is given responsibility to make sure that whatever arrangements are made are reasonable, given the size of the estate and the lifestyle of the deceased.

That's fine if the executor knew the deceased, knew his or her lifestyle, and knows what the estate contains, but what about the executor who doesn't? He or she is in a very tough spot. The executor may not know much about the estate until long after the funeral because it can take a lot of time and energy to track down all the assets of a deceased person, as we will see. Further, the executor may know nothing about how much money the deceased owes to others, nor how much of the estate will be left after those debts are paid.

The last thing an executor needs is a lawsuit by disgruntled creditors or beneficiaries who think that the executor spent too much on the funeral, or by a funeral home that didn't get paid. The most modest funeral, with casket and memorial service, costs $10 000 to $15 000. The executor who misjudges could be on the hook for significant amounts of money. It makes sense for the executor who has any doubts to be prudent and conservative.

3. What If the Deceased Made Arrangements?

The deceased may have solved the problem by purchasing a funeral plan before death. If such a prepaid arrangement is in place, then the executor has no worries. The choices were made by the deceased, not by the executor, and no matter how lavish or unreasonable the arrangements, they can proceed. Of course, most people who buy prepaid plans don't buy them to arrange lavish spectacles that will annoy their family or creditors. They buy them so that there is one less problem for the executor and the family to worry about after death, and sometimes they buy them to save the estate money because many funeral homes discount these plans.

Another option for the person who wants to save money on funeral costs, but who doesn't want to prepay the cost, is to join a memorial society. These societies exist in most cities and they make discount deals with funeral homes for their members. When the memorial society member dies, his or her executor goes to a participating funeral home to get the pre-agreed discount. Of course, this works only if the executor is aware that the deceased is a member of one of these societies and knows which funeral home to go. Also, even with the discount, the funeral expenses must still be reasonable for the size of the estate.

4. Be Careful with Headstones

A word of caution on something that many people assume is a normal part of a funeral and is automatically included in funeral expenses: grave markers or headstones. The law says that no matter what people think, these are not part of funeral costs. That means the executor does not have authority to order one or pay for it out of the estate. Of course, most people do not want the grave of a loved one to go unmarked. One thing the executor can do is tell the beneficiaries that they can buy a headstone after the estate is finalized. Another approach is to get approval for the headstone from each beneficiary in writing.

4
DUTY NUMBER 2:
FIND AND TAKE CONTROL OF THE
ASSETS OF THE DECEASED

1. Putting on the Rubber Gloves:
My Trust Company Experience

As I said in Chapter 1, it wasn't until I joined a trust company and became a trust officer that I truly understood what this part of an executor's job was all about. Specifically, my initiation came the day I was told to come to work in old clothes. I was given a box of disposable rubber gloves and warned that I would be getting very dirty. I was part of a team — no one ever went in alone, there had to be at least two people — that was going into the house of a deceased to take control of the assets.

That was also when I learned the true meaning of the word *assets*. I discovered it includes everything owned by, or owed to, the deceased — not just the obvious items like jewellery, bank accounts, investments, and houses, but, in one case I was involved in, it even included a huge collection of plastic flowers, as you will see.

The estate departments of trust companies are often referred to as "the friends of the friendless." That's because many people who appoint trust companies as executor have no one else to do the job. They often live alone. Some rely on the help of friends and family to keep going in their home, others pay for private in-home care, while others receive assistance from public health services. Still others move to seniors' complexes. Regardless of the kind of accommodation they enjoy, when they die the trust company staff must go in. Whether the home was tidy or well lived in, we always had a sensation of intruding in private spaces that contained the unique and special things that everyone accumulates over decades of normal life.

But we had a job to do. Regardless of first impressions, we always knew there was more to this person's affairs than met the eye. As I said before, trust companies do not accept an executor appointment unless the person has significant assets, because trust companies charge significant fees for this specialized work. So the estate has to be large enough, or the trust company won't agree to the job.

So when the will is made, the trust company's employees get as much information as they can about the person's affairs; but as you know, wills can sit untouched and unchanged for years, and trust company wills are no exception. Good business dictates that the company keep in touch with its clients and update their financial information regularly, but the staff cutbacks of the 1990s made that difficult. And every trust company has hundreds, if not thousands of wills in their vaults. So when a client died, we knew that we had to search very carefully to be sure we found all the assets, not just the ones of which we were aware.

2. Securing the Residence

We made our first visit to the deceased's residence as soon as we could after learning of the death, but before the funeral, if possible. That's because friends and relatives might be coming to the funeral and we wanted to make sure the home and its contents were secure. We never assumed that they might help themselves to things to which they weren't entitled, but we had a duty to make sure that didn't happen. So we checked all the locks, and if they were broken, we called a locksmith to repair them. If we weren't satisfied that we had all the keys, we would ask the locksmith to re-key the locks. Then we would take pictures of the premises, inside and out, to give us a record of the condition they were in when we took over and of what items were inside.

3. Perishable Items

We also had to check the fridge, freezer, and storage rooms for perishable foods. Anything that had been opened or partially used we threw out along with anything that would rot, such as meat, fruit, vegetables, and dairy products. Items in sealed containers (cans, boxes, plastic packs) weren't likely to deteriorate and they might be useful to a charity like the local food bank so we would leave those till later. Frozen foods were problematic. Small portions in the freezer section of the fridge we usually threw out. The contents of big freezers, however, needed more thought. If the freezer was working well and there seemed to be no risk of deterioration, we left it plugged in until we could come back and identify the contents and decide if we could find a use for them. For example, frozen turkeys might interest the local food bank. One house I remember had a storage room full of hundreds of bottles of homemade preserves. None of the jars were labelled. Since we had no idea what was in them, nor how old they were, they were thrown out.

4. Valuables That Can Walk

The next step was to go through the house to find valuables that are easily portable, such as jewellery and cash, and I was amazed at how thorough my colleagues were. They didn't just look in the obvious places like jewellery boxes, dresser drawers, or filing cabinets. They insisted we look everywhere, so we searched the pockets of garments hanging in closets, we rifled through every book and magazine, we looked behind furniture and under carpets, we went through boxes in the basement and attic, we even went through the garage or other outbuildings. We did that because we never knew when or where we would come across a diamond ring, an uncashed cheque, a savings bond, or a bundle of $100 bills. When we did find something, we put it in an envelope, which we sealed and signed, and brought it back to the office for storage in the vault.

5. Important Papers

As we searched, we also kept an eye out for important papers that would give us clues about the existence of other valuable assets such as tax returns, bank statements, life insurance policies; anything that hinted at the presence of financial assets. In particular, tax returns are a gold mine of information. They, and the reporting slips they contain, give specific details about the location of accounts or sources of the deceased's income. We would collect all this information, review it, then contact the financial institution involved to confirm that the asset had not been cashed, sold, or cancelled and to find out its value at date of death.

We also looked for utility bills, like water, heat, light, and telephone so that we could notify the utility company of the death, cancel what was no longer needed, and have future bills sent to us for payment. In the case of the telephone, we usually cancelled the service right away to prevent anyone from running up unauthorized long distance calls, though if there was a valid need to keep it going, such as a family member staying on the premises until after the funeral, we would consider leaving it until they left. In today's wired world, we often had to make a similar decision about Internet access, cell phones, or other communication devices.

6. Credit Cards

Of course, there are other portable items that cause big trouble if they fall into unscrupulous hands — credit cards. If the hospital or funeral director hadn't given us the deceased's wallet or purse already, we kept a sharp eye out for it. But we never assumed that the credit cards in the wallet were the only ones that the deceased carried. We looked for any evidence of the existence of other cards, such as statements or letters from the issuing institutions, and then we would phone to cancel the cards and ask for the balance owing.

7. Safety Deposit Box Key

Another item we looked for was a safety deposit box key and information about where the box is located. Most bank branches are very cooperative when an executor shows up with a key for one of their boxes. They usually permit the executor to open the box, go through the papers in it, remove the original will if it contains one and make a list of the remaining contents. They do not usually let the executor take out the rest of the contents at this early date. That's because the bank needs independent proof that the executor really does have authority to take control of the assets of the deceased.

8. Mail

We also went through any mail we found in the house and directed the post office to reroute all further mail to our office. Anything that looked like a flyer or unsolicited advertising we threw out but we opened all bills, bank statements, and anything else that might contain information about the deceased's assets and debts. We cancelled subscriptions to magazines, newspapers, book clubs, and so on, and asked that all further correspondence be directed to our office as executor of the estate.

9. Insurance Policies

We kept a sharp eye out for a house insurance policy. Vacant houses are at risk for break-ins and vandalism, and most policies say that if a house is going to be vacant for an extended time, the policy is void. The exact time varies; it could be 30, 60, or 90 days, and you just have to check the policy. If the house is going to be empty for longer, you have to buy extra coverage called a vacancy rider. These riders extend the insurance coverage for a longer period (the exact times vary depending on the insurance company) and they also require that the house be checked regularly by a responsible person. If a family member lived nearby, we would arrange for them to shovel snow and make sure the heat was on and the pipes didn't freeze in winter, or to cut grass in the summer, to turn lights on in the evening, to make sure the doors and windows were locked and there were no signs of unauthorized entry, and to do whatever they could to make the place looked lived in. If there were no family members nearby or available, we would hire a property management company to do that for us.

We also were on the look out for another kind of insurance policy — life insurance. The best evidence was the policy itself but we would also look for letters or statements from an insurance company. If we found something, we would contact the company to see if the policy was still in force and, if so, who the beneficiaries were. If the policy was payable to the estate, we would ask that the necessary claim forms be sent to our office. If it was payable to a named beneficiary, we would try to help the insurance company locate that person so they could make the claim.

10. Household Furnishings

As we were going through the house looking for valuables and papers we would also be paying attention to the other items in it — furniture, appliances, pictures, instruments, not to mention the contents of the bookshelves, drawers, cupboards and closets, and all the other items you find in a house. We knew that everything would eventually have to be disposed of, but the question was how? If we were lucky, the will contained specific instructions like, "I give my Heintzmann Grand Piano to my loving niece Dorothy."

11. Lists and Memoranda

Some people resist putting such gifts in their wills. They don't want to have to go to the trouble of changing the will should niece Dorothy do something to upset them and they decide to give the piano to someone else. Those people may prefer the flexibility of a list separate from the will. Called *precatory memoranda* by lawyers, these lists are often very detailed and can be a huge help to the executor. Unfortunately they are not always legally valid for one simple reason; they do not comply with the formal requirements for a will. It may seem odd to refer to these lists as wills, but because they represent a gift of property that occurs only when the person dies, that is exactly what they are. In other words, they are another type of what lawyers refer to as *testamentary instruments*, and they must be signed the way a will needs to be signed to be legal. They must be signed by the person making the will in front of two independent witnesses who are both present at the same time. In reality, they almost never are.

However, even if a list is not signed in front of two witnesses, it will still be considered valid and legally binding if it meets two conditions: it was written and signed before the will, and it is specifically referred to in the will. This happens when the will was made by a lawyer who said, "You don't want to pay me to type up a great long list of personal items that you want to leave to specific people. If you make the list and bring it in when we sign the will, I'll put a clause in the will saying that the list you made was dated and signed by you before this will and it is to be considered a part of this will for all purposes." The executor who is confronted with such a list must check the will to see if a clause like that is in it. If so, then the list is a valid and binding part of the will and the executor can do what it says.

If the list is not referred to in this way in the will, it may still be useful to the executor because it shows what the deceased person intended. The executor will be able to do what it says if he or she takes one important precaution beforehand: he or she must get agreement from all the beneficiaries. If they all agree to what the list says, then the executor can follow it. If they don't agree, then the items in the list will have to be disposed of as part of the residue of the estate.

12. Unspecified Items: To Sell or Not to Sell?

The general rule is that anything that is neither given to specific people in a will nor included in a valid and binding list is to be sold. Lawyers call this *conversion*, as in "converted into cash." But sometimes that is easier said than done. Look around your home. What real value do your lived-in furniture, out-of-date computer, and squeaky dining room set have? What about your linens, everyday plates and dishes, pots and pans, and the box of McDonald's treats-of-the-week toys that you didn't have the heart to throw out when the kids moved away?

This brings me to the plastic flowers. The first house I went into as a trust officer contained the largest collection of plastic plants and flowers I had ever seen. The living room and dining room were crammed with them. "So I guess we'll be throwing these out," I said. "Not so fast," said my colleague, who had been doing this work for many years. "They can be sold at auction." I thought she was kidding but said no more, and we checked out the rest of the house. We decided that since there was no family to pick and choose among the household goods the best way to dispose of them was to hold an auction.

When we got back to the office my colleague called a local auctioneer who met us at the house a few days later. I asked him about the plastic flowers. "No problem," he said. "We'll put them all into a couple of big boxes, and somebody will buy them." Now I knew my colleague and the auctioneer were both crazy, but he did exactly that. Out went the plastic jungle into his truck along with everything else that he deemed saleable. A month or so later we received his statement detailing the proceeds of the sale. Sure enough, there was an entry on it for the sale of two large boxes of plastic flowers. The moral of this story is twofold: don't assume that something you don't value is not valuable to the estate, and you may be able to find a friendly auctioneer to help you realize that value, for a fee of course. Another option open to the executor faced with selling the contents of a house is the garage sale, known in some parts of the country as a yard sale.

Before arranging a sale of household items that have not been given to specific people or charities in the will, you can check with the beneficiaries to see if they want anything. If they all agree, the executor can let them take what they want. Often, the executor will establish a system so that they can choose in turn; for instance, they can draw lots to see who goes first or they can go in order of age. They then go through the house and select the items that are meaningful or useful for them. After this is done, the executor still must decide whether the remaining items should be sold, given to charity, or thrown out, but there will be fewer items to deal with, and he or she will know how the beneficiaries feel about the issue. If the remaining items have value, they will probably want them sold or given to charity for re-use. If not, they should have no problem with throwing them out.

13. Vehicles

Cars and vehicles must also be inspected and stored and insurance coverage confirmed as soon as possible after the death. As executor, you should take possession of all the keys, then search the vehicles for the registration and insurance papers. You should also contact the insurance company to advise them of the death and arrange for any refund of premiums that may be due since the car will no longer be in use.

14. Contacting Banks and Financial Institutions

Armed with all the paper and information you collected during your first visit, you must then begin the task of contacting all the various agencies and institutions that hold the assets that are not physically in the house. A logical place to start is the banks and other financial institutions. A quick phone call lets them know of the death, and they will then take steps to make sure that the account isn't released to, or dealt with by, unauthorized people. For your own protection, confirm the call in writing. Your letter will serve as a record that you took the prudent steps required of you as executor, and you can also ask for the rest of the information you need.

For cash accounts, ask for confirmation of the amounts in the account at date of death. Find out whether or not interest or other amounts will accrue after death, and if so, when and at what rate. Ask what documents the institution needs to transfer control of the account into your name as executor.

For life insurance payable to the estate, ask how much is payable and what forms and documents must be submitted to make the claim. Don't forget the person's employer. There may be salary, wages, or commissions due to the deceased, and benefits such as group life insurance or pension refunds.

Get in touch with holders of retirement accounts like RRSPs, RRIFs, and the like. Find out who the beneficiaries are, and if the funds go to the estate, get information on the amounts involved and what you need to do to process the claim.

If the deceased owned stocks in publicly traded companies, you will have to get in touch with the appropriate transfer agent to arrange to have them transferred into your name as executor of the estate. Transfer agents are financial institutions, usually trust companies, that are hired by corporations to keep track of share ownership once shares are traded in the open market. Sometimes the name and address of the transfer agent is printed on the back of the share certificate. If not, call a stock broker, he or she and will tell you who to contact. While you are at it, ask the broker to confirm the value of the shares at date of death.

If the deceased owned mutual funds, find out the value of the fund at date of death and what documents and forms are required to transfer the fund into your name as executor.

The deceased may have owned Canada Savings Bonds. Review them to see when they come due. Contact the Bank of Canada to find out how much interest they have earned to the date of death. Your bank or the deceased's bank may be able to help with this.

If the deceased owned annuities, contact the issuing institution and ask if payments continue or if there is a lump sum pay-out, and determine the value of the annuity at date of death.

15. CPP, GST and OAS

Contact Canada Pension Plan (CPP) or Quebec Pension Plan in Quebec. CPP pays a one-time death benefit to the estate of everyone who paid into the CPP during their working life, but you must apply for it, so ask for the forms.

Old Age Security (OAS) benefits must be cancelled after a death. Goods and Services Tax (GST) credits are issued four times a year, and must be returned after a death.

CPP , GST and OAS payments are only entitlements to the estate if they are received during the month of death. In other words, if the deceased died in October, then any payments received from November onwards must be returned to the government, or they will be charged to the estate.

However, you can ask if there are other CPP, GST or OAS benefits payable to the surviving spouse or dependent children of the deceased. Note that for many federal government programs, the definition of spouse has expanded in recent years to include both common-law and same-sex couples. If the deceased is survived by an unmarried partner, that person may also be entitled to benefits under these programs. Make sure to ask.

16. Businesses, Land, and Rental Properties

If the deceased ran a business, you will have to take steps to keep it running until it can be sold or transferred as the will requires. If it was an incorporated business, check the company documents to see if there is a buy-sell agreement in place. If so, contact the company's lawyer or accountant to find out how to trigger that agreement. If the business is unincorporated, it could be either a sole proprietorship run by the deceased alone or the deceased could have been in partnership with others. The partners may or may not have signed a formal partnership agreement that deals with the death of a partner. Find out if there is a partnership agreement and what it says about that. If not, find out if the partners are interested in buying the deceased's share or if the partnership will be wound up.

If the deceased owned rental properties, make sure the buildings are being properly looked after, that suitable insurance is in place, and that rents are being collected.

If the deceased owned land, you must do a search of the title to confirm ownership. Check if the title is in the deceased's name only or if he or she owned it jointly with someone else. Remember there are two kinds of joint ownership and they are treated very differently when one owner dies. If the land is owned in *joint tenancy*, the share of the deceased will pass automatically to the surviving owner. However, if the land is owned in tenancy in common, then the share of the deceased does not go to the surviving owner; it goes to the beneficiaries in the deceased's will. Joint tenancy is preferred by married couples but *tenancy in common* is used by business partners who normally want their share to go to their own families, not to their partner.

17. Collections

Collections of china pieces, stamps, artwork, coins, and the like need to be carefully stored until they can be professionally evaluated and then disposed of. Even though you have arranged for the house to be inspected on a regular basis, it might be wise to remove these into safe storage to prevent loss or damage.

18. Loans Owing to the Deceased

Are there any loans payable to the deceased? He or she may have lent money to family, friends, or business partners and may have taken security for those loans like a mortgage on a property. Confirm details, ensure payments are made, and see if the debt can be called in or sold.

5
DUTY NUMBER 3:
PREPARE AN INVENTORY, VALUE THE ASSETS, AND KEEP AN ACCOUNT

As executor, it is your job to keep track of every asset in the estate and to account for every penny that comes in and every penny that goes out. To do this, you must maintain two different records: the estate account and the estate inventory.

1. Open an Estate Account

Establishing the estate account is easy. Just set up a bank account and tell the bank to open it under the name "The Estate of Mary Smith, Deceased." Tell them you will be signing as "(insert your name), Executor," and that you need a monthly statement with cancelled cheques. You can set up a new account if that is convenient, or you can continue to use an account that belonged to the deceased once you have notified the bank of the death.

Once this account is available, use it to keep track of every penny that comes into the estate and every penny that goes out — all deposits made and all cheques written. If you do that you will create a complete record of every transaction you make as executor. When you are done, the opening balance will reconcile to the closing balance, just as it would for your own cheque book. This will make it easier for you to account to beneficiaries or anyone else who demands to know what you did with the estate assets.

2. Start an Estate Inventory

At the same time, you need to start to prepare the *estate inventory*, an accurate list of all the assets in the estate and their fair market value, both as at date of death. Because it is not unusual to find additional assets as you go along, remember to update the inventory as you proceed.

3. Take Pictures

As I said earlier, it is a good idea to take pictures of the house and its contents as soon as possible after the death, preferably before anyone has had a chance to go in and disturb or remove things. This gives you a record of exactly what condition things were in when you took over, including what was there and what was not, which might come in handy if a beneficiary claims something valuable is missing. It also gives you something to work from as you begin the estate inventory so you can work in the comfort of your own home or office.

4. Evaluating Estate Assets

Making a complete list is a big job, but evaluating assets is something else again. Financial assets like bank accounts and investments are easy; just get the balances as they were at date of death from the financial institution in writing. Other assets require professional assistance. Some examples are real estate, vehicles, and household goods.

4.1 Real estate

Real estate can be valued by a realtor or can be fully appraised by an accredited appraiser depending on how much certainty you require and whether or not you want to spend money for it. Realtors do not charge for their valuations because they are hoping to get hired to sell the property. Appraisers always charge a fee and never get involved in the sale. Generally, if there is not likely to be any dispute about the value of the lands in the estate, the opinion of a realtor will be sufficient. However, if there is likely to be a dispute, it is always better to hire an independent appraiser.

4.2 Vehicles

Cars and vehicles are hard to value because so much depends on the condition of the vehicle, how well it was maintained, and the demand for that model in your local market. The best way to establish that is to scan the classified ads in your local newspaper, then take it to a dealer for an opinion. Beware of the so-called Blue Book value. That is based on the age and model, and while it may be useful for insurance purposes, it has nothing to do with the value of the vehicle in your area. Ultimately, the true value of a vehicle, as with any asset when you get right down to it, is what a willing buyer would pay for it. Make your best estimate, and if you do sell the vehicle for more than you thought it was worth, you can change your inventory to reflect that.

4.3 Household goods

Household goods are notoriously difficult to evaluate. There are personal-property appraisers who will evaluate the furniture and other valuable items for a fee but more often than not the executor's problem is not how much they are worth but how to get rid of them. I mentioned the possibility of sending them to auction before. An experienced auctioneer will quickly tell you if the items are marketable. Please take care to distinguish truly valuable items like collectibles, art, and jewellery from the ordinary things that have only garage-sale value. True valuables must be professionally evaluated and perhaps professionally sold in order to realize that value.

5. Five Reasons to Keep an Inventory and Accounts

There are four main reasons for keeping an estate inventory: for a probate application, for tax purposes, for the beneficiaries, and for the creditors. Overriding all of these is a more self-centred purpose — to protect yourself. If you are challenged you will have to show that everything in the estate has been accounted for and the assets were properly valued.

5.1 For probate fees

The inventory is used to determine the amount the clerk of the surrogate court will charge for processing a probate application. Each province sets its own probate fees, but all of them are based on the value of the estate as shown in the inventory of assets that is included with the application. To prevent executors from fudging the figures in order to get lower fees, the executor has to swear that the inventory is true before a commissioner for oaths or a notary public before the clerk will accept the application for processing. That means that you must show fair market value at date of death, with one exception. Because household goods are so difficult to value and because they are known to go down in value over time, it is common to give them a nominal value of perhaps $1.00 on a probate application. Of course, if there are any household items that have exceptionally high values like antique furniture or expensive rugs, they need to be listed individually and valued accurately.

5.2 For taxes

I discuss the taxation of estates later, but for now we can say that death triggers capital gains tax for any assets that are eligible. The big question is what assets are these? The answer is all of them except for those that are specifically exempt, or those that are left exclusively to a spouse.

The main exemptions are for cash and the deceased's principal residence; these are not subject to capital gains tax. Life insurance proceeds that go to a named beneficiary are also not included, because they are not part of the estate. Any assets left to the deceased's spouse are also not taxed, thanks to a tax-free transfer called a *spousal rollover*. This is really a tax deferral because when the spouse transfers the asset the full amount of capital gain is triggered. Other assets that are commonly left to a spouse are RRSPs and RRIFs. Typically, the deceased will have designated the spouse as beneficiary when opening the plan but these assets can also be left to a spouse in a will. Either way, they pass to the spouse tax free at death.

All other assets owned by the deceased are subject to capital gain tax, but there is one condition: there has to be a gain. That means that the asset has to have gone up in value from the date the deceased acquired it to the date of death. That's why proper evaluation is so important. The executor has to establish not only the market value at death but also the value when the deceased acquired the asset.

Some assets never go up in price, like common household goods and ordinary vehicles, so they don't often attract capital gain tax. But others do go up. Two of the most common are real estate holdings, other than the deceased's principal residence (for example, cottages and rental or investment properties), and shares or mutual funds that are not in RRSPs. Executors of estates with these assets must be especially careful to get an accurate evaluation so they don't run into trouble with the tax authorities. I will discuss this in more detail later on.

5.3 For the beneficiaries

The estate inventory provides information to the beneficiaries of the estate. The rules about how much information the executor has to give the beneficiaries vary from province to province. Some require that the beneficiaries get all information available; others say they are only entitled to receive information about the gifts they are receiving. You will have to check the details with a local lawyer. However, full disclosure can be a very prudent policy. If you keep everyone informed on everything that is in the estate, you are likely to minimize arguments or complaints. Of course, there are families who will never be happy with what the will said and what the executor is doing. If that is your situation, you will have to decide what is best in line with the specific rules in your province.

5.3a Who the beneficiaries?

An important question arises here: who are the beneficiaries? The obvious answer is the people named in the will, and if they are all alive, your job will be simple indeed. However, beneficiaries can die before the testator, and a well planned will takes that into account. All you have to do is read it to see what the alternative arrangements are and proceed. Sometimes the will names specific alternates to receive the gift of the dead beneficiary; sometimes it refers to a class of people, such as his or her children who are alive.

5.3b Per capita and per stirpes

There are also two technical expressions that lawyers use to establish alternative beneficiaries, and those expressions are *per capita* and *per stirpes*. A gift clause in a will might say "to (name of beneficiary) or his issue then alive in equal shares per stirpes." I looked up "stirpes" and discovered it is a Latin word meaning root or stem. "Issue" means everyone descended from the beneficiary; not just his children, but their children, the children's children, and so on. Per stirpes means the gift "goes down the root" like this: if the deceased beneficiary had four kids, and they are all alive at his death, then they would share the gift equally. But if one child was not alive and he left two children of his own, they would split the share of their parent, and so on. Thus, the next generation always splits the share of their deceased parent, so the gifts get smaller as they go down through the living descendants.

Per capita works differently. "Issue in equal shares per capita" means that you check to see how many issue are alive and then divide the gift equally among them, regardless of to which generation they belong. In other words, the gift does not get smaller as it goes down; each person gets the same amount.

5.3c What if there are no alternative beneficiaries in the will?

Most wills have an alternative beneficiary clause of some sort, but others do not. Do-it-yourself wills often miss this, though I have seen it left out of wills prepared by lawyers too. If the will you are looking at does not have an alternate beneficiary clause, then the general rule is that the gift falls into the residue of the estate. If the will has a residue clause, then you follow its direction. If it does not, then you must turn to the intestacy laws of your province. These laws, known as the laws for people who die without a will, also apply to gifts that do not have alternative beneficiary clauses or residue clauses.

5.3d Special status for spouses and children

As if this is not confusing enough, you must pay special attention to the spouse and children of the deceased. There are laws that protect them from being unfairly disinherited by a spiteful spouse or parent. These laws (often called the Dependants' Relief Act — see Table 1 for the name of the law in your province), give spouses and dependent children the right to make a claim against the estate for a reasonable share of the deceased's assets if they can show that the deceased failed to do so in the will.

Each province also has a matrimonial property law designed to ensure that spouses get a fair share of the matrimonial assets in the event of a divorce or separation. Executors are often surprised to learn that these laws may apply to estates in situations in which the deceased died before the divorce was finalized. In either case you should check with a lawyer.

5.3e The expanding definition of spouse

Finally, the legal definition of spouse has expanded in recent years. The federal government and some of the provinces have extended it to include unmarried or common-law spouses, and the federal government has gone further and extended spousal rights to same-sex couples.

So deciding who the beneficiaries are can be tricky. If you are executor of a will that leaves you guessing, the best advice is to talk to a lawyer who can advise you on the laws that apply in your province.

5.4 For the creditors

Finally, the estate inventory is used to satisfy the creditors of the estate. These are the people to whom the deceased owed money. If the estate is solvent — if there is enough to pay the debts with plenty left over to make the gifts to the beneficiaries — then you will have no problem.

But there are estates that are not solvent. Then the executor has to balance all the competing interests and pay the appropriate amounts to the appropriate claimants, as we shall see in Chapter 7.

5.5 For your own protection

As I said, overriding the other four reasons for keeping an inventory and accounts is a more self-centred purpose. You do it to protect yourself. If you are challenged by beneficiaries, creditors, or even the tax people, you need to be able to show that everything in the estate has been accounted for and that assets were valued appropriately. The best protection is a complete and accurate inventory and estate account.

TABLE 1
DEPENDANT RELIEF LAWS

Province/Territory	Name of law
British Columbia	Wills Variation Act
Alberta	Family Relief Act
Saskatchewan	Dependants' Relief Act
Manitoba	Dependants' Relief Act
Ontario	Succession Law Reform Act
New Brunswick	Provisions for Dependants Act
Nova Scotia	Testator's Family Maintenance Act
Prince Edward Island	Dependants of Deceased Persons' Relief Act
Newfoundland and Labrador	Family Relief Act
Northwest Territories and Nunavut	Dependants' Relief Act
Yukon	Dependants' Relief Act

6
DUTY NUMBER 4:
FIND AND PROBATE THE WILL,
IF NECESSARY

1. What If You Don't Have the Will?

It may seem odd to talk about finding a will at this point. So far I have assumed that you actually have in hand a will that names you as executor, but that may not be so. Instead, you may believe you are the executor in a will but you don't have it yet, and you may not be sure where to look. Here are some practical suggestions.

2. Calling the Lawyer

When most people think of wills, they automatically think of lawyers, and that's a good place to start. If you know the name of the deceased's lawyer, call him or her. Say that you believe you are the executor in the will, and you would like to arrange to pick it up. Don't be surprised if the lawyer hesitates. This may be the first the lawyer has heard about the death, and he or she is likely doing a quick review of his or her memory bank or computer system for details about the client. Expect the lawyer to ask for your phone number and say he or she will call you back.

Then the lawyer will search his or her records to see if he or she has a will file for the deceased. If the lawyer does, he or she will look in his or her will-storage vault to see if the original will is there and if it names you as executor. Wills, like any information in a lawyer's file, are subject to solicitor/client privilege, and even though the client who made the will is dead that privilege still exists. The only person the lawyer can give information to at this point is the named executor. If you are named as executor, the lawyer will call you back and make arrangements for you to pick it up.

If you aren't named as executor the lawyer will still call you back, but all he or she can tell you is that he or she has a will but it doesn't name you.

If the lawyer doesn't find the original will in the vault, he or she will retrieve the file from his or her closed-file storage system. That should contain notes and information about the lawyer's meetings with the client, unsigned copies of the will, and confirmation that the client took the original with him or her. When I started law practice more than 20 years ago, it was customary for lawyers to automatically store original wills in their vaults, and clients rarely questioned that. But as the years went by, more and more people expressed the desire to take the originals with them. If the copy on file names you executor, the lawyer will tell you whatever he or she can about where the will might be.

3. What If the Lawyer Didn't Keep the Will?

When my clients asked to take the original will with them, I advised them to keep the document in a safe place and to give a copy to the executor, along with information about where the will could be found. I recommended using a safety deposit box at their bank and to be sure to give the executor the address of the branch, along with detailed information about where to find the key. If you are executor of one of these organized people, then the bank is your next stop.

4. Looking for the Will

However, many clients did not follow my advice. They had their own ideas about where to store their wills, including in filing cabinets, desk or dresser drawers, china cabinets, boxes in the basement, inside books, under a mattress, or stuck in a ceiling joist in the basement. One woman even put hers in a plastic bag in the freezer. She thought that was the safest place in the house because, she said, if there was a fire, the freezer was not going to burn down. The possibilities are limited only by human ingenuity, so if you do not know the exact location of the will, you will have to be as thorough as you can be when you search the house and belongings of the deceased to find it.

5. What If You Don't Find a Will?

If after your diligent search you do not find a will, each province has a law that applies to people who die without a will. This law is often called the

Intestate Succession Act, though other names are used. (See Table 2 for the name of the law in your province.) Regardless of its name, this law says who can apply to the court to be appointed administrator of the estate and to whom the estate must go in the absence of a will. Even though the details differ from one province to another, there is a general pattern to these laws as summarized in Table 3. Spouses and children usually come first, followed by brothers and sisters, parents and other relatives, but each province has its own variations so check the law that applies to you carefully.

6. What If All You Have Are Copies of the Will?

Finally, though you may not find the original will, you may find photocopies of it. As I have said, to be a valid will, it must be signed by the testator and two witnesses, and to this point we have been searching only for the signed original. The clerk of the court will not normally accept a probate application if all you have is a photocopy of the will. However, there are rare occasions when a judge may permit that.

TABLE 2
NAMES OF INTESTATE SUCCESSION LAWS
BY PROVINCE

British Columbia	Estate Administration Act
Alberta	Intestate Succession Act
Saskatchewan	Intestate Succession Act
Manitoba	Intestate Succession Act
Ontario	Succession Law Reform Act
New Brunswick	Devolution of Estates Act
Nova Scotia	Intestate Succession Act
Prince Edward Island	Probate Act
Newfoundland and Labrador	Intestate Succession Act
Northwest Territories and Nunavut	Intestate Succession Act
Yukon	Intestate Succession Act

TABLE 3
SUMMARY OF INTESTATE SUCCESSION LAWS

If you die without a will and you have:	Your assets will go to:
A spouse only	That spouse
Children but no spouse	Those children equally
A spouse and children	Your spouse (who gets a defined amount) and the remainder is divided among the spouse and children as the provincial law directs
	Exceptions: In PEI and Newfoundland and Labrador, assets are split equally among your spouse and children
	In Manitoba, all goes to your spouse
No spouse or children	Your closest living next of kin starting with your parents;
	if neither are alive, then your brothers and sisters or their children;
	if none of them are alive, then any other next of kin;
	if none of them are alive, then the provincial government

For example, I once submitted a probate application with the original will, but somehow it got lost at the court house. I asked a judge what to do, and he told me to submit a photocopy of the lost will in a sworn affidavit. In the affidavit he told me to explain what happened and to confirm that the copy was identical to the lost original, which it was. The judge then issued a probate certificate for the true copy. Obviously, this was an exceptional situation. If you think that there is a good reason for the court to accept a photocopy of a will for probate, you should get help from a good estate lawyer.

7. You Have the Will but Do You Need Probate?

Assuming that your search pays off, you now have the original will of the deceased, which names you as executor. Now you must decide whether or not you need to apply for probate. As I said earlier, probate means asking a judge to certify that the will you have is the true last will of the deceased. A probate certificate, in other words, gives you official confirmation of your status as executor and full legal power to do what the will says.

However, a probate application takes time and costs money. How much money depends on the size of the estate, and the province you are in. As you can see in Table 4, each province sets its own fees, and while they vary, they always get paid out of the estate, which reduces the amount available for the beneficiaries. No wonder people are always looking for legitimate ways to avoid the cost of probate. They want to make sure as many of their assets as possible go directly to their friends or family without paying these fees. If all the deceased's assets do this, then you obviously don't need to get probate. One of your jobs as executor is to determine whether the deceased's assets do or do not require probate.

8. Two Kinds of Assets That Do Not Need Probate

There are two types of assets that do not require probate: *joint with right of survivorship assets* and *designated beneficiary assets*.

The most common joint assets are cash assets and real estate. Cash assets include bank accounts, term deposits, and even Canada Savings Bonds. As for real estate, the family home is the most common asset that is jointly owned. It used to be the case that only married couples owned assets jointly, but that is no longer so. Now, non-married and same-sex couples often have joint assets, and other people may also. For example, after the death of the spouse, an older parent may set up joint accounts with one of his or her grown children, who can then help with the banking and other chores. However, as I said earlier, there are two kinds of joint ownership in law, and the difference is critical when one joint owner dies. It is worth reviewing here.

TABLE 4
PROBATE TAX RATES BY PROVINCE

Province or Territory	Total gross value of the estate	Probate tax rate	Probate tax on a $500 000 estate
British Columbia	Under $10,000 $10,001 and higher Plus if $25,000 to $50,000 Plus for each $1,000 over $50,001	zero $208 $6 per $1,000 $14 per $1,000	$208 + (25 x $6) + (450 x $14) = **$6,658**
Alberta * Alberta calculates its probate tax on the net value of the estate after the debts are subtracted.	Under $10,000 $10,001–$25,000 $25,001–$50,000 $50,001–$100,000 $100,001–$250,000 $250,001–$500,000 $500,001–$1,000,000 Over $1,000,001	$25 $100 $200 $400 $600 $1,500 · $3,000 $6,000	**$1,500**
Saskatchewan		$7 per $1,000	**$3,500**
Manitoba	Under $5,000 Plus for each $1,000 over $5,001	$25 $6 per $1,000	$25 + (495 x $6) = **$2,995**
Ontario	Up to first $50,000 Plus if over $50,001	$5 per $1,000 $15 per $1,000	(50 x $5) + (450 x $15) = **$7,000**
New Brunswick	Under $5,000 $5,001–$10,000 $10,001–$15,000 $15,001–$20,000 Plus for each $1,000 over $20,001	$25 $50 $75 $100 $5 per $1,000	$100 + (480 x $5) = **$2,500**
Nova Scotia	Under $10,000 $10,001–$25,000 $25,001–$50,000 $50,001–$100,000 $100,001–$150,000 $150,001–$200,000 Plus for each $1,000 over $200,001	$75 $150 $250 $500 $600 $800 $5 per $1,000	$800 + (300 x $5) = **$2,300**

TABLE 4 — Continued

Province or Territory	Total gross value of the estate	Probate tax rate	Probate tax on a $500,000 estate
Prince Edward Island	Under $10,000 $10,001–$25,000 $25,001–$50,000 $50,001–$100,000 Plus for each $1,000 over $100,000	$50 $100 $200 $400 $4 per $1,000	$400 + (400 x $4) = **$2,000**
Newfoundlandand and Labrador	Under $1,000 Plus for each $1,000 over $1,000	$80 $5 per $1,000	$80 + (499 x $5) = **$2,575**
Northwest Territories and Nunavut	Under $500 $501–$1,000 Plus for each $1,000 over $1,001	$8 $15 $3 per $1,000	$15 + (499 x $3) = **$1,512**
Yukon	Under $10,000 $10,001–$25,000 Plus for each $1,000 over $25,000	Zero $140 $6 per $1,000	$140 + (475 x $6) = **$2,990**

The first kind of joint ownership is called *tenancy in common*. In this kind of joint ownership each person, called a tenant in common, owns a specific share of the asset, say 50/50, though the proportion can vary according to the agreement between them. When one tenant in common dies, that 50 percent share goes to the beneficiaries in his or her will, if there is one, or to the default beneficiaries listed in provincial law if there is no will.

The other kind of joint ownership — the one in which we are interested — is called *joint with right of survivorship*. With this kind of joint ownership the law pretends that each owner, called a joint tenant, owns 100 percent of the asset simultaneously. When one joint tenant dies, the other already owns the whole asset, so it all goes to him or her regardless of what the will of the deceased or the law of default beneficiaries says.

Designated-beneficiary assets are those that allow a person to choose a beneficiary to receive the asset when the owner dies. The most common examples are life insurance, registered savings plans such as RRSPs and RRIFs, and employer pension plans. Anyone who has purchased one of these or signed up for a new job that has a pension plan will remember being asked to name a beneficiary and will remember that there was no formality involved in signing the form. However, these forms create a gift that only occurs at death, so you may wonder why they do not have to be signed with the same formality as a will — in front of two independent witnesses. The simple answer is that the law specifically exempts them from the signing requirements for wills as a matter of convenience.

The important thing is for you to be aware of these differences, and when you find a jointly owned asset, to confirm the type of joint ownership. If all the assets in the estate are joint with right of survivorship or designated-beneficiary assets, then you will not need to get probate. Ownership of the assets will pass to the joint owner or the designated beneficiary automatically.

9. How Probate Protects the Executor

Another reason why you might decide to get probate is to protect yourself. As we have seen, an executor is responsible to a number of people, about many of whom he or she may not know anything. Any one of them could sue the executor if he or she was inadvertently left out of the estate. Fortunately for the executor, the probate process is designed with a number of built-in protections for the executor. If followed, these protections ensure that the executor can finalize the estate without fear that an unknown party will come forward with a claim against him or her. The most important of these are advertising for creditors, issuing notices, and passing accounts.

9.1 Advertising for creditors

The procedure called advertising for creditors allows the executor to run an ad in the local paper calling on anyone who is owed money by the deceased to come forward within a fixed period of time or lose the right to make a claim.

9.2 Issuing notices

The probate process requires that the executor serve notice on spouses and dependents of the deceased if it seems that they might be able to make a claim under the family relief laws and the matrimonial property laws of each province.

9.3 Passing accounts

A procedure called passing accounts allows the executor to present his records of the estate to a judge for approval. Once granted, the executor is free from claims by the beneficiaries and the creditors.

Note: Details of these procedures vary from province to province. For specific information, talk to a good estate lawyer in your area.

10. Probate Confirms the Will Is Valid

A third reason for getting probate is when there are questions about the validity of the will. For example, someone might say that the deceased was not of sound mind when he or she signed the will. Or there might be an allegation that the deceased was pressured into signing the document against his or her free will. Another allegation is that the will was not signed in accordance with the formalities; perhaps the two witnesses did not sign in front of the deceased and each other. If any of these are proven, the will is invalid and the executor's appointment is nullified. There could also be more than one will, as in the Howard Hughes situation mentioned earlier, which can lead to a court action to determine which one is the true last will. In all of these situations, it will be necessary to take the problem before the appropriate court so a judge can decide if the will is valid or not. If any of these situations arise, get the advice of a good estate lawyer.

11. Avoiding Probate in Small, Cash-Only Estates

Finally, there is one more situation where probate might not be necessary, and that is when the estate is small and the assets are mostly personal effects and a small bank account or two. Think of the elderly person who lives in a small rented apartment on Old Age Security and perhaps a modest pension from work. Even though this person may have a will naming you executor and none of his or her assets are jointly owned with anyone, you still may not need to get probate of the will to handle the estate. That's because the banks may allow you to take control of the accounts if the amounts involved are small enough. The exact figure varies from bank to bank, so check with the one that has the account to see if this is possible.

If the amount is small enough, the bank will need some papers signed before you can take control of the account. The bank will ask you to sign a form called an *indemnity*, which says that the bank will release the money to you as long as you agree to cover the bank for any expenses that arise if anyone else comes along claiming the right to handle this estate. It will also ask the beneficiaries to sign a release. These say that the beneficiaries agree that the money can be turned over to you without probate and they will not sue the bank if for some reason it is determined that you were not entitled to receive it.

7
DUTY NUMBER 5:
DEAL WITH DEBTS AND CLAIMS
AGAINST THE ESTATE

Estate debts can be divided into three categories: debts relating to the death, debts of the deceased, and debts incurred by the executor to handle the estate.

1. Debts Relating to the Death

These are funeral and burial expenses and, as we already discussed, they are payable out of the estate as long as they are reasonable in light of the standard of living of the deceased. It is your job as executor to make sure of that, and you must not let the wishes of family or friends distract you. If you overspend, you may have to pay back any excess amounts out of your own pocket. Remember that grave markers are not included. If you wish to order one, make sure you have written consent from all the beneficiaries first, and that there will be enough left in the estate to cover the debts. If not, you could be making up the cost of the grave marker yourself.

As a practical matter, many funeral homes offer a discount if you pay the bill within a limited period of time, but that time may be short. You probably don't want to pay the bill out of your own funds, but how do you pay it with the deceased's money if you don't have access to his or her bank account? Fortunately, the law provides a solution. It says that funeral and burial expenses take priority over any other debts. As a result, if you take the funeral bill to the bank, they will issue a draft payable to the funeral home right out of the deceased's account.

2. Debts of the Deceased

Almost everyone who dies owes money to somebody. Even a person who lives in a paid-up house and never uses credit cards owes money for utilities and similar services. Your job as executor is to unearth details of everything the deceased owes and pay it. If you don't, you could end up paying those debts yourself, out of your own pocket.

2.1 Looking for debts

We have already talked about what you need to do to dig up those debts. You have to look in every nook and cranny where the deceased might have put information about them. Every box, drawer, cupboard, and filing cabinet is fair game. Remember that you are also looking for papers that will point you in the direction of debts, papers like cheque-book records, cancelled cheques, and bank statements. Don't forget the home computer. Many people use software programs to keep track of their affairs. They can log on to the bank website and download up-to-the-minute details of their accounts and holdings at any time of day or night. If the deceased owned a computer, check it for one of these programs.

You may find papers that point you to other people who know something about the deceased's debts, people like accountants, brokers, bankers, insurance agents, financial planners, and lawyers. If so, contact them to see what information they have for you.

2.2 Business or partnership debts

Perhaps the deceased owned a business. If so, you will have to find out if he was sole owner or if there were partners or other shareholders. If he was sole owner, the deceased is personally responsible for its debts, so you will have to take control of the business to avoid running up more debts until you can sell it or close it down.

If the business was a partnership or a corporation there may be, as I said earlier, a contract covering what happens to the deceased's share of the business after death. In the case of a partnership, it is called a partnership agreement, for corporations it will be either a buy-sell agreement or a unanimous shareholders' agreement. Search through the deceased's records for a copy, or ask the lawyer or the accountant who looked after the affairs of the business for one. Review the contract and follow the procedure it sets out for disposal of the deceased's share of the business.

2.3 Medical bills and claims by caregivers

There may be bills owing for medical services given to the deceased that are not covered under the provincial health-care plan, or under any supplementary health insurance that the deceased might have had. One common example is ambulance fees for the last trip to hospital.

If the deceased was in a nursing home or similar facility, there will likely be an outstanding bill for the last month of residence. There may also be bills owing to private caregivers — people hired to come into the nursing home, or the deceased's residence, to give the deceased extra care and attention.

Problems arise when caregivers claim that the deceased promised them something from the estate but there is nothing to back that up. They might claim that the deceased obviously forgot to change the will to take care of it, and they are entitled to something anyway, out of fairness. These claims arise more often than you might think, and they raise some complicated legal issues. If you are faced with this situation, consult a lawyer.

2.4 Insured debts

Some debts may be insured, like a house mortgage, a credit card debt, or money borrowed from the bank on a line of credit. Check with the lending institution to see if there is insurance, and if so, make the claim and get the debt paid off.

2.5 Advertising for creditors

As I said earlier, some executors are confident that they know all the details of the financial life of the deceased. Perhaps they are closely related to the deceased and were handling his or her affairs for some time before death. Those fortunate executors are not worried about finding debts that they never heard of before. But other executors are not so lucky. They are not familiar with the deceased's affairs. They may not have known they were graced with the job of executor until they were contacted after the death. Even after a thorough search of the deceased's home they still can't be sure they found everything.

These are the executors who need to advertise for creditors of the deceased. Details of this are different from province to province, but the idea is the same everywhere. To advertise for creditors, you place a notice in the local paper advising anyone to whom the deceased owed money that they have a fixed number of days to bring you details of their claim. If they do not, then they will be barred from making that claim in the future, and you can proceed with the handling of the estate without worrying about anyone coming out of the woodwork and catching you by surprise.

I used to wonder why there are more obituaries in the paper than there are notices to creditors of deceased persons. Once I began doing estate work, I discovered that a big reason was the cost of placing these notices in the paper. They are expensive, so executors try to avoid running them if they can. Nonetheless, any executor who is not sure that he or she has found all the debts of the deceased should run one. The cost is always a legitimate expense payable by the estate.

2.6 Challenging claims by creditors

Once you have received all of the creditors' claims, you must review them and decide if they are payable or not. If you have doubts about any of them, there is usually a procedure that allows you to force the claimant to provide proof of its claim within a fixed number of days. If they do not, then you can ignore it. If they do, then a judge rules on it and you proceed accordingly. Details of this procedure vary, so check with a good estate lawyer in your province.

2.7 Child or spousal support

Less obvious debts that might come up include ongoing child support or spousal support. Sometimes these payments stop at death; sometimes they do not. To be sure, you must check the agreement that was signed when the spouses divorced, or other legal papers that established responsibility for the child in question. Since these obligations can be substantial and can last for a long time, the best idea is to have those papers reviewed by a good family lawyer.

2.8 Leases and mortgages

If the deceased owned or rented real estate you will have to check to see if he or she is still responsible for the rent or the mortgage. Residential leases can often be terminated on fairly short notice after a death, but the rules vary from province to province so you will have to check locally. Leases on commercial property are different. They are usually for a fixed number of years and they usually say they are binding on the estate of the deceased. Get a lawyer to look at the document and advise you on your options.

2.9 Lawsuits against the deceased

Another unexpected debt occurs when the deceased is the subject of certain lawsuits. The most common example is when the deceased died in a motor vehicle accident that he or she caused and for which he or she may be legally liable. If you think that the estate may be faced with a liability of this sort, talk to a lawyer.

2.10 Unenforceable debts

You must also watch for debts that are not collectible. One example is a debt that is so old it exceeds the time limit set out in a law called the statute of limitations. Another example is a debt based on an obligation that is so personal to the deceased that it cannot be performed by anyone else. For example, if I died before finishing this book, the publisher could not sue my estate to get the book finished. Our contract, though valid, would be unenforceable. If you face any situations like these, contact a lawyer.

2.11 Claims by spouse or children for more of the estate

Finally, I have already mentioned the possibility that the estate might be subject to claims by the spouse of the deceased or by his or her dependents under the family relief and matrimonial property laws of the province. These also give rise to complicated legal issues so if they come up in the estate you are handling you should get legal help.

2.12 Paying debts

Once you have decided which debts are payable, you must check the will to see if specific assets are set aside for payment of them. For instance, when land is subject to a mortgage, it is assumed that the land is the primary source of payment of the amount owing. Another example is when the deceased foresaw that cash would be needed to pay debts, so he or she bought a specific insurance policy to cover them. If not, then the rule is that all the assets in the estate are available for payment of debts. The executor must sell the assets, pay the debts out of the cash, and divide the remainder among the beneficiaries as designated in the will. Problems arise when there is enough cash for the debts but not for the beneficiaries, or when there is not even enough money for the debts.

2.12a Enough for the debts but not for the beneficiaries

If there is enough to pay the debts but there will not be enough left to satisfy each beneficiary in full, contact a lawyer. There are complicated rules that decide how the beneficiaries will share the remainder.

2.12b Not enough for the debts

If there is not even enough money in the estate to pay the debts, then the estate is insolvent and the beneficiaries will get nothing. There are complicated rules on which debts take priority and get paid before others. If the estate you are handling is insolvent see a lawyer.

It is interesting to note that the laws on bankruptcy apply to estates as well as to people, so another option is to put the estate into bankruptcy. A licensed bankruptcy trustee would take over and sort things out, for a fee of course. Putting an estate into bankruptcy makes sense when there are very large amounts of money at stake, or complex legal issues that need to be addressed.

2.13 One creditor always comes first

Please note there is one debt that takes priority over almost all others, and that is the debt we owe to the Canada Revenue Agency (CRA), which we commonly refer to as income tax. I talk about the various tax consequences of death in Chapter 8. Here, I just want to point out that you may assume that a notice to creditors published in your local newspaper will protect you or the estate from claims by our friends at the cra, but it is not so. They are in a very special position when it comes to getting paid. While they do not step ahead of a secured creditor, like a bank that has a mortgage on a house, and they won't get paid if the estate is truly insolvent (if there really is no money and no assets to turn into money, nobody will get paid), they do come before any other debts except funeral expenses. And they don't have to reply to a notice to creditors either. So if you hand out estate assets without first clearing up any unpaid taxes, cra will come after you personally for the money. Ignore them at your peril.

2.14 Keeping the house going

Any services that are still necessary, such as heat and power until the house can be emptied and sold, for example, must be continued. You will have to arrange for those bills to be sent to you as executor of the estate. Others that are not needed, including newspaper and magazine subscriptions and the like, should be cancelled to prevent unnecessary charges.

3. Debts Incurred by the Executor

It is inevitable that you will incur some expenses as you go through the process of handling and finalizing the estate. For example, you may make long distance phone calls to family and friends of the deceased to advise them of the death or to keep them informed of your progress. You may run up significant mileage on your car as you drive around looking after things. These could be trips to the bank, to an insurance office, to a financial advisor or stock broker, to various government offices, not to mention numerous trips to and from the home of the deceased. If the deceased owned property out of town, like a cottage or a farm, you may need to drive out there to keep an eye on things.

Also, even though funeral expenses are payable by the estate and the banks do make efforts to get them paid out of the deceased's funds, there may be times when you need to advance money out of your own pocket to cover funeral expenses.

Remember you are entitled to reimburse yourself for any expenses you incur to do your job as long as those expenses are reasonable given the size of the estate. However, you cannot simply write yourself cheques as soon as the bank gives you control over the deceased's accounts. The law does not permit executors to draw any funds for themselves without first accounting for them to the beneficiaries. That means you must prepare a list of the expenses you incurred and send it to all the beneficiaries for review. You will include a release for them to sign saying that they are satisfied with the expenses and they authorize you to pay yourself for them. This is normally done at the end of the estate, when the executor is sending them his or her accounts for all the estate assets. Sometimes, however, an executor who is out of pocket for very large amounts will ask for reimbursement before the estate is finalized.

If the estate includes a business owned by the deceased, it may continue to run up expenses until you are able to deal with it. If you can, you will sell it and put the sale proceeds in the estate account, but this takes time, and many small, one-person businesses do not have much resale value when their owner/operator dies. If it can't be sold as a going concern, then all you can do is sell off the assets of the business for the best price you can get. If the business is a partnership or a corporation with more than one shareholder, then there may be a contract, variously called a partnership agreement, a buy-sell agreement, or a unanimous shareholders' agreement that kicks in when one owner dies. If so, all you have to do is facilitate the transfer of the deceased's share to the other owners. Either way, you may incur expenses as you look after this, and these too are reimbursable from the estate.

Finally the deceased may die in the middle of something that takes money, such as building a new home or cottage. You will have to use your best judgement and decide whether or not to complete the project or to sell it as is. Remember that if you make a decision that costs the estate money, then the beneficiaries can come after you for the loss. If you have any doubts about this or any other aspect of your job as executor, contact a good estate lawyer.

8
DUTY NUMBER 6:
PAY ANY TAXES OWING BY THE
DECEASED AND THE ESTATE

As the cliché goes, there are two things we can't avoid in life — death and taxes. Unfortunately, when you put the two together you get "death tax," and that expression upsets and befuddles people more than any other subject in the realm of estates. That's because people think that the government automatically takes a percentage of everything they own when they die. The good news is that is not true. It used to be true, but that kind of death tax hasn't existed in Canada since 1972.

1. Capital Gains Tax

The bad news is that when the classic death tax was thrown out, the government replaced it with another tax, called *capital gains tax*. Canada's government seems to have a knack for replacing a narrow tax that only applies to one situation with a broader tax that applies to many situations. That is true with capital gains tax: not only is it triggered when we die but it also applies at certain times while we are alive too. For our purposes, all you need to know as executor of an estate is that capital gains tax is triggered by death.

The most important thing to remember about capital gains tax at death is that it is only payable if the deceased owned the kinds of assets that attract it. Even then, the tax is only payable if those assets have gone up in value since the deceased acquired them. The kinds of assets that attract this tax are called *capital assets*. The most common capital assets that you find in the estate of ordinary Canadians are land and buildings, stocks and bonds, and mutual funds.

Cash or assets that are quickly convertible into cash, such as term deposits, guaranteed investment certificates, and Canada Savings Bonds, are not included in the definition of capital assets; therefore they are not subject to capital gains tax. That's because cash assets earn interest, which is included in the deceased's income and taxed each year. In contrast, increases in the value of capital assets don't get reported and taxed every year. That only happens when the deceased does something with the asset that triggers capital gains tax, like sell it.

So here's how the capital gains tax works. When someone dies, the law pretends that they sold all their capital assets for fair market value immediately before they died. In tax language this is called a *deemed disposition*, which means "a pretend sale." As executor, it is your job to get reasonable independent evidence of what that pretend sale price would likely be by contacting skilled appraisers or others familiar with market conditions at the time of the death.

Then you must determine the original value of the asset when the deceased acquired it. Usually, that value is the price he or she paid for it, though sometimes a deceased may receive an asset as a gift. You may find evidence of the original value in the deceased's records but if not, you may have to get an expert to help you reconstruct the value at that time. In any event, this value is called the *cost price*.

If the asset is a building, and if the deceased spent money on improvements to it, you may be able to add those costs to the cost price to arrive at a higher figure called the *adjusted cost base* for the asset. However, the rules on this are complicated, and if you think it applies to an asset in your estate, you should contact a good accountant.

To calculate the amount of the gain, you simply subtract the cost price of the asset (or the adjusted cost base if it applies) from the current market value of the asset. But you are not done yet. The next step is to determine how much of that gain is taxable and must be included in the deceased's income for the year of death. To do that you must know the *capital gain inclusion rate*, which is set by the government from time to time. The good news is that this rate has been going down in recent years.

For many years the inclusion rate was 75 percent, but in 2001 the federal government reduced it, not once but twice! First they dropped it to 66 2/3 percent, and then they dropped it further to 50 percent. So, for someone who dies now, one-half of the gain on their capital assets is taxable.

For example, assume that the deceased owned a small strip mall. He paid $300,000 for it in 1978 and he spent $200,000 in allowable improvements. He died in January 2002, and a certified real estate appraiser tells the executor that the property is then worth $1,000,000. The gain on this property is $500,000, and the amount to be included in the deceased's income is $250,000, calculated as follows:

Fair Market Value	$1,000,000
Less Adjusted Cost Base	- 500,000
Equals Capital Gain	= 500,000
x 50% Inclusion Rate Equals amount to include in deceased's income	$250,000

A strip mall, of course, is a type of real estate. While not many Canadians are fortunate enough to own one, many of us do own another kind of real estate: our homes. Imagine the amount of tax that the government would take in, and the corresponding loss to future generations, if everyone had to include the gain on their homes in their income at death. Fortunately, the government exempted homes from this tax back in 1972 by what is called the *principal residence exemption*. To my knowledge, there has never been a proposal to change that, probably because the entire country would rise up in protest. So unless you hear otherwise, as executor, you can rest assured that the deceased's home is exempt from capital gains tax.

But this is not so for the family cottage or other recreational properties. These are taxable, and you must take steps to value them and include any gain in the deceased's income. Also, the law says that a person can have only one principal residence at a time, and while a cottage can become a principal residence in the right circumstances, the rules for declaring that are complicated. If you have any doubt about the status of real estate in the estate you are looking after, get the advice of a good lawyer or accountant.

There is another exemption that might be available if the deceased owned a farm or a small business. Basically, if this exemption applies, the first $500,000 of value will be exempt from tax; however, the rules governing this are very complicated. You should consult a tax lawyer or an accountant if you think this might be relevant to the estate you are looking after.

2. Tax Deferrals and Rollovers

Death can also have an important tax impact in another way. It can start in motion, or bring to an end, a tax benefit called a *tax deferral*. As the name implies, a tax deferral is a legal way of deferring, or postponing, tax on assets until the occurence of some future event.

Death begins a deferral and postpones tax that would otherwise be payable, when the deceased leaves assets exclusively to his or her spouse. Called a *spousal rollover* in tax jargon, the collection of tax is left to a later date, usually when the surviving spouse dies.

A spousal rollover occurs in two ways, when the deceased's will leaves assets to the spouse by way of an outright gift, or when the will puts assets in trust for the spouse. However, a spousal trust only qualifies for the tax deferral as long as the spouse is the only one who can receive benefits under that trust. If the trust allows assets to be used for the benefit of others, such as the children of the deceased, the trust is called a *tainted spousal trust* and the tax free rollover is lost. Similarly, if the trust gives the executor power to decide who will benefit from the assets, the rollover is not available. If you are executor of an estate, get legal advice to confirm whether gifts to a spouse or in trust for a spouse qualify for this rollover.

As I said earlier, the federal government recently changed the definition of spouse to include not only common-law couples but also same-sex couples, and many provinces are following suit. This means that the surviving partner in these relationships should receive the same treatment for tax purposes as a legally married widow or widower. The law in this area is changing rapidly, so if the deceased lived in one of these relationships, get legal advice to make sure you are aware of the latest developments.

There is another rollover that applies only to estates containing farms. If the farm or the shares of a farm corporation are left to a child who continues to farm, then no tax is payable. The rules are complex and the area is specialized. If this comes up, talk to a lawyer or accountant who is well versed in tax law as it applies to farming.

Death can bring an end to a tax deferral that is used by countless Canadians to reduce taxes while they are alive, and that is the well-known retirement savings plan called the RRSP. As you probably know, money invested in an rrsp grows tax free until the plan is cashed in, is converted to another plan to provide retirement income, or until the person dies. At death, all the income that built up in the plan tax free must then be taxed. That is done by adding it to the deceased's final tax return.

Those who have spouses can avoid that by using the spousal deferral we just discussed. If they leave the RRSP to a spouse, then the money is transferred tax free into the RRSP of the spouse and tax on it is deferred until the spouse dies or otherwise deals with the plan in such a way as to trigger tax.

There are also some situations in which rrsp funds can be transferred to the children and even the grandchildren of the deceased on a tax free deferral basis. However, the rules are complicated, so if you have any questions about the tax treatment of an RRSP in an estate you should talk to a lawyer or accountant.

If there is no deferral, then there is a question about who pays the tax that comes due on the RRSP. We know that the deceased can name a beneficiary of the RRSP when he or she buys the plan, or that can be done in a will. But who pays the tax? Is it the responsibility of the beneficiary so that it gets paid out of the plan or is it payable by the estate out of other assets?

You might think it fair that he who gets the benefit pays the price, but not necessarily so. The law assumes that in the absence of anything to the contrary in the deceased's will, the tax is payable by the estate. If the will doesn't say anything or if it says taxes are paid by the estate, that's what happens. If the will says that taxes are to be paid out of the RRSP before it is transferred to the beneficiaries, then that is what you must do. The best advice is to check the will closely before you do anything, and if you have questions, check with a tax lawyer or an accountant.

The law also says that the estate and the beneficiaries are jointly liable for tax on these plans. If tax isn't paid by the estate, the government can go after the beneficiaries, but that is small comfort to you as executor because the government can come after you too. Get good advice on your particular estate before you do anything.

3. Tax-Free Assets

Fortunately, there are some assets that don't attract any tax at all on death. As I said, cash, or assets that are readily convertible into cash, such as gics, term deposits, and Canada Savings Bonds, are common examples.

The other common tax-free asset is life insurance. I'm not sure why, perhaps the life insurance industry has an exceptionally powerful lobby in Ottawa. Whatever the reason, 100 percent of the proceeds of a life insurance policy get paid to the beneficiaries named in that policy. No tax is taken off and none is owed. This makes life insurance a very valuable estate planning tool. If you can purchase it, you can use it to leave a large cash gift to loved ones, or you can buy it to offset a large tax liability, like a capital gain, that will come due on your death. The insurance industry offers a number of products that do this.

Of course, once the cash gift or the life insurance money is invested by the beneficiaries, they will have to report the income earned by those funds and pay tax on it every year.

4. Tax Returns at Death

Death truly is a mystery. It raises spiritual and philosophical questions that have intrigued humans for centuries. Tax law is also a mystery. It has befuddled Canadian executors since it was introduced as a temporary measure during the First World War.

No executor is surprised to learn that he or she must file returns for and pay tax owing by the deceased up to the date of death, but many are unaware that death creates another taxable entity: the deceased's estate. The law says that the estate, which comes into existence at the moment of death, is a trust, and like any other trust it is taxable.

As executor, you will have to report income for two time periods. First, you have to report the deceased's income from the last return he or she filed to the date of death. Second, you have to report the estate's income from the date of death to the date you distribute the estate as directed by the will and as required by law. If you don't, and if taxes are owing, then the government will come after you for that money.

5. Returns for the Deceased

5.1 The terminal return

You must file a tax return to cover the deceased's income for the year of death — income earned from the first of January to the actual date of death. This return is normally called the *terminal return* but there is no special form for it. When you ask cra for the terminal package for a deceased person, they give you the same package of forms that you use for your own personal taxes, the T1 Income Tax and Benefit Return (see Sample 1 — the form may look different depending on your province).

However, to make sure that CRA knows that you are submitting a terminal return for someone who died that year, you must do the following:

On the first page of the T1 form:

(a) Make it clear you are filing for a deceased person. Under the box headed "Identification" the form asks for a name. Enter: "The Estate of [name of deceased], Deceased," or "The Estate of the Late [name of deceased]." But underneath the name, give your address so the cra will send future correspondence to you and not to the residence of the deceased.

(b) Give the province of residence of the deceased in the box headed "Information About Your Residence."

(c) Give the social insurance number, date of birth, and marital status of the deceased on December 31 of the previous year, in the box headed "Information About You." (**Note:** Give only the deceased's information, not yours.) For "language of correspondence" indicate your preference as cra will be corresponding with you.

(d) Enter the date of death in the box that says, "if this return is for a deceased person, enter the date of death."

(e) Sign your name and then print "executor" in the signature box on the last page.

To confirm your status as executor you must also include —

• a copy of the death certificate, and

• a copy of the will naming you executor.

To prevent any possibility of confusion, include a covering letter with the return explaining that you are filing as executor of a deceased person.

Otherwise, complete the rest of the return using the information you have about the deceased's income. Note that even though this return is only for part of a year, the part from January 1 to the date of death, the CRA lets you claim a full year's tax credits for the deceased. For help with this, and most of the other questions that commonly arise, get a copy of the CRA's free guide called *Preparing Returns for Deceased Person* (T4011).

SAMPLE 1
INCOME TAX AND BENEFIT RETURN
CRA T1 GENERAL 2006

Canada Revenue Agency — **Agence du revenu du Canada**

T1 GENERAL 2006
Income Tax and Benefit Return
Complete all the sections that apply to you in order to benefit from amounts to which you are entitled.

8

Identification

Attach your personal label here. Correct any wrong information.
If you are not attaching a label, print your name and address below.

First name and initial

Last name

Mailing address: Apt No – Street No Street name

PO Box | RR

City | Prov./Terr. | Postal code

Information about you

Enter your social insurance number (SIN) if you are not attaching a label:

Enter your date of birth: | Year | Month | Day

Your language of correspondence:
Votre langue de correspondance : | English | Français

Check the box that applies to your marital status on December 31, 2006:
(see the "Marital status" section in the guide for details)

1 ☐ Married   2 ☐ Living common-law   3 ☐ Widowed
4 ☐ Divorced 5 ☐ Separated   6 ☐ Single

Information about your spouse or common-law partner (if you checked box 1 or 2 above)

Enter his or her SIN if it is not on the label, or if you are not attaching a label:

Enter his or her first name:

Enter his or her net income for 2006 to claim certain credits: (see the guide for details)

Enter the amount of Universal Child Care Benefit included in his or her net income above (see the guide for details):

Check this box if he or she was self-employed in 2006: | 1 ☐

Information about your residence

Enter your province or territory of residence on **December 31, 2006:**

Enter the province or territory where you **currently** reside if it is not the same as that shown above for your mailing address:

If you were self-employed in 2006, enter the province or territory of self-employment:

If you **became** or **ceased** to be a **resident of Canada in 2006**, give the date of:

entry | Month | Day   or   departure | Month | Day

Person deceased in 2006

If this return is for a deceased person, enter the date of death: | Year | Month | Day

Do not use this area

Elections Canada

THIS SECTION APPLIES ONLY TO CANADIAN CITIZENS.
DO NOT ANSWER THIS QUESTION IF YOU ARE NOT A CANADIAN CITIZEN.

As a Canadian citizen, I authorize the Canada Revenue Agency to provide my name, address, and date of birth to Elections Canada for the National Register of Electors. .... Yes ☐ 1 No ☐ 2
Your authorization is required each year. This information will be used only for purposes permitted under the *Canada Elections Act*.

Goods and services tax/harmonized sales tax (GST/HST) credit application

See the guide for details.
Are you applying for the GST/HST credit? .... Yes ☐ 1 No ☐ 2

Do not use this area | 172 | | | 171 | | | |

5000-R

SAMPLE 1 — Continued

2

Your guide contains valuable information to help you complete your return.
When you come to a line on the return that applies to you, look up the line number in the guide for more information.

Please answer the following question:

Did you own or hold foreign property at any time in 2006 with a total cost of more than CAN$100,000? (read the "Foreign income" section in the guide for details) .... **266** Yes☐ 1   No☐ 2
If *yes*, attach a completed Form T1135.

If you had dealings with a non-resident trust or corporation in 2006, see the "Foreign income" section in the guide.

As a Canadian resident, you have to report your income from all sources both inside and outside Canada.

Total income

Employment income (box 14 on all T4 slips)	**101**	
Commissions included on line 101 (box 42 on all T4 slips) **102**		
Other employment income	**104 +**	
Old Age Security pension (box 18 on the T4A(OAS) slip)	**113 +**	
CPP or QPP benefits (box 20 on the T4A(P) slip)	**114 +**	
Disability benefits included on line 114 (box 16 on the T4A(P) slip) **152**		
Other pensions or superannuation	**115 +**	
Universal Child Care Benefit (see the guide)	**117 +**	
Employment Insurance and other benefits (box 14 on the T4E slip)	**119 +**	
Taxable amount of dividends (eligible and other than eligible) from taxable Canadian corporations (see the guide and **attach** Schedule 4)	**120 +**	
Taxable amount of dividends other than eligible dividends, included on line 120, from taxable Canadian corporations **180**		
Interest and other investment income (**attach** Schedule 4)	**121 +**	
Net partnership income: limited or non-active partners only (**attach** Schedule 4)	**122 +**	
Rental income Gross **160** Net **126 +**		
Taxable capital gains (**attach** Schedule 3)	**127 +**	
Support payments received Total **156** Taxable amount **128 +**		
RRSP income (from all T4RSP slips)	**129 +**	
Other income Specify:	**130 +**	
Self-employment income (see lines 135 to 143 in the guide)		
Business income Gross **162** Net **135 +**		
Professional income Gross **164** Net **137 +**		
Commission income Gross **166** Net **139 +**		
Farming income Gross **168** Net **141 +**		
Fishing income Gross **170** Net **143 +**		
Workers' compensation benefits (box 10 on the T5007 slip) **144**		
Social assistance payments **145 +**		
Net federal supplements (box 21 on the T4A(OAS) slip) **146 +**		
Add lines 144, 145, and 146 (see line 250 in the guide). = ▶ **147 +**		
Add lines 101, 104 to 143, and 147. This is your **total income. 150** =		

SAMPLE 1 — Continued

> **⬉ Attach your Schedule 1 (federal tax) and Form 428 (provincial or territorial tax) here. Also attach here any other schedules, information slips, forms, receipts, and documents that you need to include with your return.**   3

Net income

Enter your **total income** from line 150.   150 | |

Pension adjustment
(box 52 on all T4 slips and box 34 on all T4A slips)   206 | |

Registered pension plan deduction (box 20 on all T4 slips and box 32 on all T4A slips)	207	
RRSP deduction (see Schedule 7 and **attach** receipts)	208 +
Saskatchewan Pension Plan deduction (maximum $600)	209 +
Annual union, professional, or like dues (box 44 on all T4 slips and receipts)	212 +
Child care expenses (**attach** Form T778)	214 +
Disability supports deduction	215 +
Business investment loss Gross **228** Allowable deduction	217 +
Moving expenses	219 +
Support payments made Total **230** Allowable deduction	220 +
Carrying charges and interest expenses (**attach** Schedule 4)	221 +
Deduction for CPP or QPP contributions on self-employment and other earnings (**attach** Schedule 8)	222 +
Exploration and development expenses (**attach** Form T1229)	224 +
Other employment expenses	229 +
Clergy residence deduction	231 +
Other deductions Specify:	232 +

Add lines 207 to 224, 229, 231, and 232. 233 = ► ▬

Line 150 minus line 233 (if negative, enter "0"). This is your **net income before adjustments**. 234 =

Social benefits repayment (if you reported income on line 113, 119, or 146, see line 235 in the guide) 235 ▬

Line 234 minus line 235 (if negative, enter "0"). If you have a spouse or common-law partner, see line 236 in the guide.
This is your **net income**. 236 =

Taxable income

Canadian Forces personnel and police deduction (box 43 on all T4 slips)	244	
Employee home relocation loan deduction (box 37 on all T4 slips)	248 +
Security options deductions	249 +
Other payments deduction (if you reported income on line 147, see line 250 in the guide)	250 +
Limited partnership losses of other years	251 +
Non-capital losses of other years	252 +
Net capital losses of other years	253 +
Capital gains deduction	254 +
Northern residents deductions (**attach** Form T2222)	255 +
Additional deductions Specify:	256 +

Add lines 244 to 256. 257 = ► ▬

Line 236 minus line 257 (if negative, enter "0")
This is your **taxable income**. 260 =

Use your taxable income to calculate your federal tax on Schedule 1 and your provincial or territorial tax on Form 428.

Refund or Balance owing

4

Net federal tax: enter the amount from line 50 of Schedule 1 (**attach** Schedule 1, even if the result is "0")	420		
CPP contributions payable on self-employment and other earnings (**attach** Schedule 8)	421 +		
Social benefits repayment (enter the amount from line 235)	422 +		
Provincial or territorial tax (attach Form 428, even if the result is "0")	428 +		

Add lines 420 to 428.
This is your **total payable** 435 =

Total income tax deducted (from all information slips)	437	•
Refundable Quebec abatement	440 +	•
CPP overpayment (enter your excess contributions)	448 +	•
Employment Insurance overpayment (enter your excess contributions)	450 +	•
Refundable medical expense supplement	452 +	•
Refund of investment tax credit (**attach** Form T2038(IND))	454 +	•
Part XII.2 trust tax credit (box 38 on all T3 slips)	456 +	•
Employee and partner GST/HST rebate (**attach** Form GST370)	457 +	•
Tax **paid** by instalments	476 +	•
Provincial or territorial credits (attach Form 479 if it applies)	479 +	•

Add lines 437 to 479.
These are your **total credits** 482 = ▶ –

Line 435 minus line 482 =

If the result is negative, you have a **refund**. If the result is positive, you have a **balance owing**.
Enter the amount below on whichever line applies.

Generally, we do not charge or refund a difference of $2 or less.

Refund 484 _____ •   **Balance owing** (see line 485 in the guide) 485 _____ •

Amount enclosed 486 _____ •

Direct deposit – Start or change (see line 484 in the guide)

You do not have to complete this area every year. Do not complete it this year if your direct deposit information for your refund has not changed.

Refund and GST/HST credit – To start direct deposit or to change account information only, **attach** a "void" cheque or complete lines 460, 461, and 462.

Notes: To deposit your CCTB payments (including certain related provincial or territorial payments) into the **same** account, also check box 463.
To deposit your UCCB payments into the **same** account, also check box 491.

Attach to page 1 a **cheque** or **money order** payable to the Receiver General. Your payment is due no later than April 30, 2007.

Branch number	Institution number	Account number	CCTB	UCCB
460 _____ (5 digits)	461 _____ (3 digits)	462 _____ (maximum 12 digits)	463 ☐	491 ☐

I certify that the information given on this return and in any documents attached is correct, complete, and fully discloses all my income.

Sign here

It is a serious offence to make a false return.

Telephone ___ – ___ – ___   Date ___

490 **For professional tax preparers only**

Name: ___
Address: ___

Telephone: ___ – ___ – ___

Do not use this area	487 ☐	488 ☐						

Privacy Act Personal Information Bank number CRA/P-PU-005

It is available at your local cra office or you can get it from their website at www.cra-adrc.gc.ca. You can also get help from an accountant.

Keep in mind the deadlines for filing this return and for paying any taxes owing by the deceased. If the deceased died between January 1 and October 1, the terminal return must be filed and any tax owing must be paid by April 30 of the year after death. But if the deceased died in November or December, the deadline for filing and payment is six months after the date of death.

If you are late, CRA can charge a late-filing penalty (currently 5 percent of the amount due) plus they can charge interest at 1 percent per month. However, if you feel that the return is late for reasons that were beyond your control, you can send CRA a letter explaining the situation. If they accept your explanation, they have the power to cancel these late charges.

5.2 Three optional returns

For reasons that I have never understood, the law allows an executor to file more than one return for a deceased person if the deceased has certain kinds of income. This is good because when it is possible the deceased pays less tax than if all his or her income was included on the terminal return. Here's why.

As we all know, Canada uses a graduated tax system, which means that the amount of tax payable increases as our income rises. Currently, federal tax rates go up in four steps:

- 16 percent on income of $30,754 or less
- 22 percent on income between $30,755 and $61,509
- 26 percent on income between $61,510 and $100,000
- 29 percent on income of $100,001 or more

For example, if you earn $50,000, you pay 16 percent federal tax on the first $30,754 and 22 percent on the rest as follows:

$$\$50,000 - \$30,754 = \$19,246 \times 22\% = \$4,234$$
$$\$30,754 \times 16\% = \$4,921$$

Total federal income tax $9,155

But because the executor can report the deceased's income on separate tax returns, the tax payable can be lowered in two ways: one, a lower tax rate might apply to the income claimed on that optional return; and two, the executor can claim some or all of the deceased's personal tax credits on each return.

The rules governing these optional returns are complicated. For more information, refer to the CRA guide that I mentioned earlier or see an accountant. However, for our purposes, here is a brief summary of these optional returns and when they are available.

5.2a Optional return 1: The rights and things return

The law calls some types of income that a deceased might receive *income from rights or things*, but that merely begs the question, what is a right or thing? Basically, rights and things are amounts that would have been taxable income and included in the deceased's return if he or she had lived for the whole year, but which had not yet been received by the deceased before death.

As an example, think of dividends on corporate stocks. One reason you buy stocks is to receive dividends, which are paid out of the company's profits once or twice a year. If the deceased owned any stocks that paid dividends, and a dividend had been declared but not paid before he or she died, then that amount qualifies as a right or thing. It can be included in a rights and things return for the deceased and does not have to be included in the terminal return. This means that the dividend amount is taxed at a lower rate, and in this case the law lets the deceased claim full personal tax credits on the rights and things return, which reduces the tax owing even more.

Another example of an amount that qualifies as a right or thing is uncashed but matured bond coupons. There are others, but they are technical. If you encounter assets that might qualify as rights and things, get advice from an accountant.

5.2b Optional return 2: Business income return for partner or proprietor

If the deceased was a partner in a business, or was the sole owner operator of a business, this optional return will be available if the business has a year end other than December 31 and the deceased died before December 31 but after the end of the business's fiscal year.

For instance, many businesses have a fiscal year end of March 31. If the deceased died on May 30, you can file this optional return to cover his or her income from the business for the period April 1 to date of death rather than put it on the terminal return.

5.2c Optional return 3: Testamentary trust income return

This is available if the deceased was receiving income from a trust that was set up in someone else's will, if that trust has a year end that does not fall on December 31, and if the deceased died after the trust's year end.

For example, the deceased received money from a trust set up by his late mother in her will. The year end of that trust is March 31, and the deceased died May 30. You can file this optional return to cover the income from that trust for the period April 1 to date of death of the deceased. If you think this applies to the estate you are handling, check with an accountant.

5.3 Claiming credits on optional returns

Some tax credits can be claimed on each optional return, some can be divided among the optional returns you are filing, and some can only be claimed against specific types of income that are related to the credit claimed, so they must be claimed on the return that shows that income.

Credits claimable in full on each return include the usual personal credits (the basic personal amount, plus amounts for age, spouse, or dependents if applicable). The credits that can be split among optional returns include disability credits, education deductions, charitable deductions, and medical expenses. Credits that can be only claimed against related income include rrsp deductions, union or professional dues, cpp contributions, and ei premiums. For a complete list, see the guide referred to earlier and if you have concerns talk to an accountant.

6. Unfiled Returns for the Years before Death

Some executors find that the deceased has not filed tax returns for a number of years. Others, finding that the deceased's records are not in good order, may wonder if this is the case. Of course, Canadian law says that no one has to file a tax return if he or she doesn't have any taxable income, but most low-income people file anyway to get tax-related benefits like GST rebates.

However, if the deceased in your case did not file and you think he or she might have been taxable, you can't just turn a blind eye to the situation. If you do, you may be on the hook for any unpaid amounts. To find out if the deceased is up to date, contact cra and ask. If not, you can file returns for the missing years as well.

7. Returns for the Estate

7.1 T3 return for the estate

As I said, the law considers the estate of the deceased to be a trust and the executor the trustee responsible for it. After the death of the deceased, until the estate is wound up and distributed to those entitled to it, the estate will earn income and that income is taxable, but not in the hands of the deceased. That is because trusts are considered to be separate taxable entities, so this income does not go on any of the returns discussed above. Instead, the cra has a special return for trusts called a T3 and a free information guide called *The T3 Trust Guide*.

The kind of income that the estate will earn after date of death includes interest on bank accounts, the cpp death benefit if the deceased is eligible for it, any death benefits paid by the deceased's employer, any salary owing from date of death to the end of the month of death, and any refund of pension contributions.

No personal credits apply to T3 returns, but there is a $10,000 credit available against death benefits from employers, and the four graduated tax rates also apply.

T3 returns must be filed 90 days after the year end of the trust. In the case of an estate, the executor can choose any date up to one year after the death. Most executors choose the anniversary of the death as year end so the T3 is due 90 days after that.

7.2 T3 return for any trusts in the estate

If the will of the deceased sets up trusts for others, like the deceased's spouse or children, these trusts can file their own T3 returns for the income they earn after date of death. For some reason this is not commonly done, but it could result in lower taxes due to the application of the graduated rates we have already discussed. If you think this can be done in your case, talk to an accountant.

8. Tax and the beneficiaries

If you are thinking that all these tax returns are well and good but you know of several estates for which the only tax return filed by the executor was the T1 terminal return, you would be right. That is a perfectly legal choice in simple estates — estates in which all the assets are going directly to adult beneficiaries who all live in Canada. However, that does not mean that cra turns a blind eye to the income earned by the estate from date of death until the date the beneficiaries receive their cheques. As we already know, cra looks to the executor for any unpaid tax, and tax on estate income is no exception.

In these simple estates the executor is acting on faith. He or she is hoping that the beneficiaries will divide that income pro rata and include their share on their tax returns for the year in which they receive it. To let CRA and the beneficiaries know that this is the plan, the wise executor includes a cover letter explaining that when he or she files the T1 terminal return and sends copies to each beneficiary. Later, when the reporting slip arrives for that income, the executor should send a copy of it to all beneficiaries with a note reminding them to include their share of that income on their personal return.

9. Clearance certificates and holdbacks

By this point, you are probably wondering what you, the executor, can do to keep yourself out of trouble with the CRA. If you are like most people, you want something in writing confirming that you filed everything you need to file and paid all the taxes the estate needs to pay. And you would like to have that before you send any money to the beneficiaries, even though the beneficiaries are wearing you out with their phone calls, wondering what is taking you so long.

Fortunately, CRA understands your concerns and they will give you that letter, called a *clearance certificate*, once they have everything they need. Sample 2 is the form you use to request a clearance certificate.

In a perfect world, you will promptly file all the necessary returns, cra will send you a notice of assessment, which you can pay and cra will send you a clearance certificate so you can safely distribute the rest of the estate to the beneficiaries. And all this will happen within a month or so of the death, right?

TX-19 ASKING FOR A CLEARANCE CERTIFICATE

Canada Revenue Agency | Agence du revenu du Canada

ASKING FOR A CLEARANCE CERTIFICATE

Use this form if you are the legal representative for an estate, business, or property and you are asking for a clearance certificate. A legal representative includes an executor, administrator, liquidator, trustee, or like person other than a trustee in bankruptcy.

Send this form to the Assistant Director, Audit, at your tax services office. Do not attach this form to the return. You can find the address of your tax services office on our Web site at www.cra.gc.ca/contact or in the government pages of your telephone book.

Do not send us this form until:

- you have filed all the required tax returns and have received the related notices of assessment; and
- we have received or secured all income taxes (including the provincial or territorial taxes we administer), Canada Pension Plan contributions, Employment Insurance premiums, and any related interest and penalties.

DO NOT USE THIS AREA

Attach to this form the documents listed below to help us issue the certificate without delay:

- a copy of the will, including any codicils, renunciations, or disclaimers, and all probate documents (If the taxpayer died intestate, also attach a copy of the document appointing an administrator and details of the proposed distribution of assets. Include the name, address, and social insurance number or account number of each beneficiary and his or her relationship to the deceased.);
- a copy of the trust document;
- a statement showing the properties and the distribution plan, including the date chosen for the distribution of properties, and a list of the recipients of each of the properties (for each property, provide a description, the adjusted cost base, and the fair market value at the date of death or distribution);
- any other documents that are necessary to prove that you are the legal representative; and
- a letter of authorization that you have signed if you want us to communicate with someone else.

For more information, get Information Circular 82-6, *Clearance Certificate.*

Identification area

Name of deceased, corporation, or trust, whichever applies

Address

Social insurance number, trust number, or Business Number, whichever applies | Date of death **or** date of wind-up, whichever applies

Legal representative's name (if there is more than one, please provide the details on a separate sheet)

Legal representative's address (we will send the clearance certificate to this address)

Legal representative's capacity (for example, executor, administrator, liquidator, or trustee) | Telephone number ( )

Period covered

I am asking for a clearance certificate for the period ending _____

Tax returns filed

Have you filed any tax returns for the year of death? ☐ Yes ☐ No

If *yes*, indicate what type of tax return(s) you filed. For more information, get guides T4011, *Preparing Returns for Deceased Persons,* T4012, *T2 Corporation Income Tax Guide,* and/or T4013, *T3 Trust Guide.*

☐ T1 final return ☐ T1 return for rights or things ☐ T2 Corporation Income Tax Return

☐ T1 return for income from a testamentary trust ☐ T1 return for partner or proprietor ☐ T3 Trust Income Tax and Information Return

Certification and undertaking

I am asking for a clearance certificate from the Minister of National Revenue. The certificate will certify that all taxes (including provincial or territorial taxes administered by the Canada Revenue Agency), Canada Pension Plan contributions, Employment Insurance premiums, and any related interest and penalties for which the deceased, corporation, or trust named above is liable (or can reasonably be expected to become liable) have been paid or that the Minister has accepted security for the amounts. The certificate will apply to the tax year in which the distribution is made and any previous year for which I am liable (or can reasonably be expected to become liable) as the legal representative of the deceased, corporation, or trust identified. I will complete the distribution of all of the property as soon as possible after I receive the clearance certificate.

_____ | _____ | _____
Date | Capacity (for example, executor, administrator, liquidator, or trustee) | Signature

_____ | _____ | _____
Date | Capacity (for example, executor, administrator, liquidator, or trustee) | Signature

TX19 (07)
Printed in Canada

(Français au verso)

Canada

Those of you who have been involved in estates before can be forgiven for chuckling. You know that these things take time, more time than you originally thought, and far more time than the beneficiaries think reasonable. Getting a clearance certificate from the hard-pressed folks at cra can take months, and it is not unusual for a year to pass before the executor is ready to distribute.

To speed things up, many executors distribute estate assets in two stages by making use of what is called a *holdback*. It works like this. When the executor is confident of the approximate amount of tax owing by the deceased and the estate, he or she doubles or triples that amount and holds it back in the estate account. The balance gets handed out to the beneficiaries. Later, when all the returns are filed, the taxes are paid, and the clearance certificate arrives, the executor can safely release the rest. If you think this might be appropriate in your case, discuss it with an accountant.

Note: There are other important documents that must go to the beneficiaries whenever you release money or assets to them and these are discussed in Chapter 9.

10. Goods and Services Tax at Death

The GST comes into play at death in two situations. First, if the deceased was receiving the GST credit, he or she would normally receive those cheques four times a year (July, October, January, and April). If the death occurred in the month before these cheques are issued, you must send it back. If the death occurred during one of these months or in the month following, then the payment belongs to the estate of the deceased. In that case, CRA requires that you send the cheque back with a covering letter confirming the death, and they will reissue the cheque in the name of the estate.

Second, if the deceased was a GST registrant — someone who carried on a business for which he or she had a GST number and who paid GST as required — you, as executor, step into the deceased's shoes and some very complicated rules come into play.

Basically, if you carry on the deceased's business activities, you must continue to charge and remit GST. When you distribute the assets that were used to run the business, the GST registration is cancelled, and a final GST return must be filed and any tax owing must be paid. There is one exception: when the assets used for the business are going to a beneficiary who is also a GST registrant and who will use those assets to carry on the business, then a rollover happens and no gst is due.

Either way, you can apply for a clearance certificate confirming that all tax is paid. Also, as usual, if you do not comply and GST is owing, you as executor become liable for any unpaid amounts.

If the deceased was a GST registrant who ran a business, the best advice is to talk to an accountant or estate lawyer who has specialized gst knowledge before doing anything.

9
DUTY NUMBER 7:
ACCOUNT TO, AND GET RELEASES FROM,
THE BENEFICIARIES

1. Why You Must Keep Accounts

The law says that an executor must constantly be ready to account for his or her handling of the assets in an estate. Most executors know that they have to keep thorough accounts that are always up to date; however, most executors aren't sure why. They think that the surrogate court will be closely supervising everything they do and will want to see their accounts on a regular basis, but nothing could be farther from the truth. In the vast majority of estates, the surrogate court never sees any accounts.

2. It's a Self-Policing System

Why do executors need to keep accounts if the surrogate court doesn't want them? The answer is simple. As an executor, you must keep accounts because your job isn't finished — and your liability hasn't ended — until you show the accounts to the beneficiaries and the beneficiaries provide their written approval. That's because the estate-management system is self-policing. Here's how it works.

The executor gets probate from the court and takes control of the deceased's assets. He or she pays the debts and taxes and eventually is ready to distribute the remainder of the estate to the beneficiaries as required by the will. Up to this point, if no one has challenged what they are doing, most executors will have had no further contact with the surrogate court. They certainly will not have filed any accounts for the estate.

3. What the Beneficiaries Want

Before you distribute the remaining assets to the beneficiaries, you need to know that the beneficiaries are happy with the job that has been done. For their part, the beneficiaries want to know that you did your job properly so they won't be on the hook for anything you missed. They want to know that you —

- paid all the deceased's debts and taxes,
- paid reasonable amounts for funeral and related expenses,
- earned an appropriate amount of interest on the estate accounts and investments,
- gave designated items to the people specified to receive them, and
- propose a fair and accurate division of the remainder of the estate as required by the will.

The beneficiaries also want to know what amounts you intend to pay yourself, as a fee for the work done and as reimbursement for any out of pocket expenses that you incurred while handling the estate.

4. What the Executor Wants

As executor, you want something back from the beneficiaries — written confirmation that they are satisfied with your handling of the estate and accounts. You also want assurance that the beneficiaries won't change their minds and complain about any of these things in the future. In order to make this clear, you send another form along with the accounts called a release. The release says that the beneficiaries accept the amounts shown in the accounts as full satisfaction of what they are entitled to in the will and that they give up the right to sue the executor in the future.

If the beneficiaries are happy with the accounts, they sign their approval, sign the release, and return these documents to you. When you have received signed approvals and releases from all of the beneficiaries, you write the cheques or release assets to them. All this happens without one page of accounts being filed at the surrogate court.

5. What Unhappy Beneficiaries Can Do

If a beneficiary is not happy with the accounts, he or she will not sign these forms. Instead, he or she will ask the executor for an explanation. The executor, who has a complete and up-to-date set of accounts, can show what has been done and the beneficiary may be satisfied.

However, if a beneficiary is not satisfied with the accounts, he or she has the right to ask the court to review the situation. Then the executor must file his or her accounts with the surrogate court and be prepared to defend them in a formal hearing. Incidentally, this can happen at any time during the handling of an estate. A beneficiary who suspects that the executor is not doing the job does not have to wait for the executor to produce accounts. Instead, the beneficiary can demand them, and if they are not satisfactory the beneficiary can ask the court to review the conduct of the executor. Each province has its own rules about the format of estate accounts. If you do have to file yours with the surrogate court, check with them to find out what their requirements are.

6. Protect Yourself with Good Accounts

The real reason you must maintain thorough and up-to-date accounts is to protect yourself. In the ordinary course, the only time the beneficiaries in most estates see those accounts is when you send them out for approval before distributing the assets. However, as executor, you must always be ready for a challenge, and keeping good accounts is the best defence.

7. Beneficiaries Hate Silence

Speaking from years of experience as an estate lawyer and then as a trust officer, I know that what troubles beneficiaries the most is the long period of silence while the executor goes about his or her work. Sometimes, especially if relations among the beneficiaries are sour, an executor may have the feeling that the beneficiaries are lurking out there waiting for a chance to pounce, and that they are given that chance when the executor sends out the accounts.

To avoid a last-minute ambush, consider being proactive. Send out information to the beneficiaries as you go along. Make it clear that it is preliminary information that will change but let them know that you will do whatever you reasonably can to keep them informed as you progress. Doing so gives them the chance to speak up earlier if they do have a concern, it should show them that you do have their best interests at heart, and it might help them understand the challenges you face, even in a simple estate. It also might save you the stress of having to go over everything in front of a judge, and save the estate the legal costs that always go along with a court procedure.

8. The Beneficiary Who Won't Sign but Does Nothing Else

A different situation arises when a beneficiary is unhappy, refuses to sign the forms, but also refuses to do anything else about it. This beneficiary just sits there as if hoping that his or her intransigence will lead the executor to give him or her more money out of the estate. Meanwhile the other beneficiaries sign and return their forms.

The formal option for this executor is to make his or her own application to the surrogate court to have his or her accounts reviewed and approved by a judge. This decision is good because once a judge approves the accounts, the executor is free to distribute the remainder of the estate without the signature of the recalcitrant beneficiary. But it is also bad because of the delay it causes, and because there will be legal costs to pay, even if they are charged against the uncooperative beneficiary.

This very thing happened on a file in which I was involved. I was acting as the lawyer for an elderly woman who was executor of her sister's estate. The will left a sum of money to a relative who could politely be described as the black sheep of the family. The executor warned me that he had a nasty temper and would likely be difficult, and she was right. A few days after we sent out the accounts and releases to the beneficiaries, he called my office. He treated me to a tirade of foul language, the gist of it being that he wasn't happy with the amount, he wasn't signing anything, and we could take him to court for all he cared.

This call was the most abusive I had ever had in my career as a lawyer, and I was sure that the executor would be as upset as I was when I reported it to her. To my surprise, she just laughed. She said that was exactly what she expected him to do and I wasn't to worry about it because his bark was much worse than his bite.

I told her that the proper legal step was to make an application to the surrogate court to have her accounts reviewed and approved by a judge. I said that I was confident that the judge would see that there was nothing wrong with her accounts and then charge the legal costs to the relative's share of the estate, but it would still take time and money to get this done.

She laughed again and said that would not be necessary. I'll never forget the determination in her voice as she said, "Let's call his bluff. He isn't going to risk one penny of his precious money on taking me to court. Besides, he's lucky to be getting anything, and he knows it!" We distributed the money, sent him a cheque, and a few days later it came through, endorsed and cashed. We never heard another word from him.

The lesson is that an executor who is certain that his or her actions have been correct and will withstand judicial scrutiny can take the chance and distribute the estate without the signature of a stonewalling beneficiary, and without court approval. Nonetheless, if this situation arises, get advice from a good estate lawyer first. You need to know exactly what risk you are taking if the worst happens and that beneficiary takes you to court later on.

9. Your Executor Fees

As executor, you are entitled to charge a fee for the work you do. That fee is payable out of the estate and it must be included in the accounts that you send to the beneficiaries. If I know one thing about executors' fees it is this: beneficiaries always think the fees are too high, and fees are often a source of trouble.

The reasons for this are perfectly understandable. First, beneficiaries usually have no idea how much work you are doing on their behalf. Second, until they receive your accounts they will not have a clue what you are going to charge for your fees, or how your fees will be calculated. Third, the format of the accounts puts the fee right up against the amounts that go to the beneficiaries themselves and makes it easy for them to say that you are taking away too much of their money.

10. Avoiding Trouble over Executor Fees

Therefore, it is a good idea to assume that you will be questioned about your fees. Be ready to show that what you ask for is fair and reasonable. Keep a detailed log of the time you spent on the estate and be precise about what you did. Keep track of all the time spent going through boxes and papers, cleaning out the house, organizing the sale of unwanted household items, trips to the bank, the broker, the dump, everything. As part of the entry showing your fees, show how many hours you spent.

11. Calculating Your Fee

How are executor's fees calculated? As a rule of thumb, 3 percent to 5 percent of the value of the estate is considered reasonable for most estates, and two provinces, British Columbia and Prince Edward Island, have set a maximum of 5 percent. However, whether there is a maximum or not, the law of each province says that any executor's fee must be fair and reasonable in proportion to the size of the estate and the amount of work done by the executor.

12. Setting a Reasonable Fee

If the beneficiaries are unhappy with your fee, and if you cannot satisfy them by explaining what you did to justify it, they will refuse to approve the accounts and they will not sign the release. Then you must go to the surrogate court to ask a judge to review and approve your accounts. The judge will look at the following factors to decide if your fees are reasonable or not:

- Size of estate
- Care and responsibility required by the executor
- Amount of time involved
- Skill and ability of the executor
- Degree of success the executor had in settling the estate quickly, efficiently, and properly

However, if on second thought you see that your fees are a bit unreasonable, you can revise your claim and go back to the beneficiaries with the lower number. If they are happy, they will sign off, you get the protection you want and no money is spent on going to court. I am not saying that it is acceptable to use the accounts as a way of negotiating your fee, but I am saying is that the setting of executor's fees is more an art than a science, and there is always room for discussion on what is reasonable in any given estate, so be prepared for that. If you keep the factors listed above in mind as you go about your work, you should have no problem with your fee later on.

13. Some Executors Don't Charge a Fee

Please note, not every executor always charges a fee. When I was in practice I was amazed at how many executors took on this onerous job and saw it through without ever asking for so much as a penny for their efforts. They were the good hearted folks who did the job out of a sense of family duty or out of loyalty to a friend. The executors who did charge a fee, in my experience, were those who were not close to the deceased, or those who were given complicated estates that consumed inordinate amounts of their time. However, the fact remains that every executor is entitled to claim a fee if he or she wishes.

14. Can You Charge a Fee If You Also Receive a Gift?

There is some ancient English case law that says if an executor receives a gift in a will, he or she cannot then charge for the work he or she does looking after the estate unless the will specifically permits a fee. Even though this law is a couple of centuries old, some lawyers believe it still applies to modern times. The situation arises often; it is very common for a beneficiary to be named as executor in a will that says nothing about charging a fee. To avoid any conflict or confusion, and before you take any fees, always disclose the amount you are claiming to the beneficiaries. If all the beneficiaries agree to the proposed fee in writing, you will have no problems with it.

10
DUTY NUMBER 8:
DISTRIBUTE TO THE BENEFICIARIES

Once the approvals of accounts and signed releases have arrived from each and every beneficiary, or once you have a court order approving your accounts, you are free to distribute the estate assets to the people entitled to them in the will.

1. Conversion to Cash or Distribution in Specie

The will usually specifies which items, if any, must be given to certain people. If not, the rule is that the executor must *convert the assets*, which means he or she must turn them into cash, and divide the money. However, most wills have a clause in them that allows the executor to distribute some assets in specie, which means they can be handed over as they are. This clause is usually found at the back of the will in the section that lists the executor's powers. It allows the executor to give beneficiaries items of equal value without going to the trouble of selling them, especially if the beneficiaries would rather have the item itself.

For instance, the estate might include a boat, a car, and a trailer all of similar value. If there are three beneficiaries who each want one of these items, and if the will has a clause allowing distribution in specie, the executor can give each of them the item they want and avoid the trouble and cost of a sale. As always, you should consult a lawyer before doing this.

2. Missing Beneficiaries

A different problem arises if you can't find one of the beneficiaries. There are private companies that specialize in searching for lost beneficiaries who can assist you. However, if the beneficiary can't be found after all your efforts, you might have to go to court for a declaration that the beneficiary is presumed dead. Then you can distribute his or her portion as the law of your province allows. The law is different in each province, so if this occurs consult a lawyer.

3. Deceased Beneficiaries

If a beneficiary is not alive when the person who wrote the will dies, check to see if the will says what is to happen to that deceased beneficiaries share. A good will covers that situation. If the will doesn't, then the gift may become part of the residue of the estate, or it may pass to the family of that deceased beneficiary by virtue of other laws. If you are faced with this situation you should contact a lawyer.

Another problem occurs when one of the beneficiaries dies while you are looking after the estate. If that happens, the general rule is that the share that beneficiary would have received goes to his or her beneficiaries. Obviously that means you have to find the executor of the deceased beneficiary's estate, be satisfied that it is all right to give the share to that executor, and be sure that if you do hand the assets over you will not be challenged for that later. By now you know that the best proof that you are the executor is a probate certificate. If the person claiming to be the executor of the deceased beneficiary can't produce one, or if you have doubts about the documents he or she does produce, contact a lawyer.

Now that we have examined the eight duties of an executor in some detail, let's look at what an executor does, and how these eight duties apply, in two typical estates.

Part III
TWO TYPICAL ESTATES

11
APPLYING THE EIGHT DUTIES TO
TWO TYPICAL ESTATES

Now we will see how Sam Smith learned what being an executor was about, not just once but twice. The two estates that he had to look after arose out of the deaths of his wife Mary and his widowed mother Sally. They are typical of the estates that I saw when I was in law practice. Even though these are fictional stories, they will give you an idea of what real people must do when they have to act as executor of an estate.

I tell the story of these estates in chronological order, just the way they would normally happen. At the end of each story, I explain how what was done relates to the eight duties of the executor that we discussed in the last eight chapters. In both estates, the eight duties are not followed in strict numerical order but they are all accounted for. That is normal. Events in real life never seem to follow a logical sequence, and estates are no different. As you will see, in the first estate, three of the duties are not relevant at all.

1. Estate 1: Mary Smith — Sam's Wife and Mother of Their Children

Sam and Mary Smith had the happiest of lives, a perfect house, two nice cars, a motor home, and two terrific kids. Every weekday morning, Sam would kiss Mary goodbye and drive off to his great job. Mary would bundle up the kids and drive them to school. Then she would drive to one of her many volunteer commitments in the community. Sam was fond of saying, "It doesn't get any better than this!" And he was right.

But it all ended the day the truck driver didn't see Mary. After dropping off the kids at school, she waited for the light to turn green then drove through the intersection. The trucker, fumbling for his cell phone that had fallen to the floor, didn't see the red light nor did he see her pull out. He hit her broadside.

A staff member at the emergency department of the hospital found Sam's business card in Mary's purse and called the number. He told Sam to hurry over. Sam was too late. The emergency doctor took Sam aside and gave Sam the news. Mary was dead.

Sam was devastated. He simply couldn't imagine life without Mary. But then he thought of the children and he knew one thing; he had to keep going for their sakes.

The first decision was in many ways the hardest. The hospital staff wanted to know where to send the body. Sam had never dealt with funeral homes before so he had no idea what to say. Friends who had recently been through the loss of a parent recommended the one they had dealt with, so he chose it. He went there after leaving the hospital. He was surprised at the cost of funerals, but he knew that Mary carried a small insurance policy "just in case," so he made arrangements.

When he got home, Sam realized he had no idea what to do next. He knew Mary had a will — they both did wills when their first baby was born — and he knew it left everything to him and made him executor, but he had no idea what an executor was supposed to do. So Sam did what many people do in this situation: he called the lawyer. That turned out to be a very helpful call.

The lawyer offered his condolences and then told Sam not to worry. He confirmed that Mary's will did leave everything to Sam and did appoint Sam as executor; but more important, ownership of most of their assets would transfer automatically to Sam at the moment Mary died. Of course, there was some legal paperwork to be done, the lawyer said, such as getting Mary's name removed from the title to their home, but that could wait. The most important thing right now was the funeral and the family, the lawyer told Sam. Call in a few weeks to discuss what had to be done, he said.

Sam was greatly relieved to hear this, and a few weeks after the funeral, Sam called the lawyer and made an appointment. When they met, they reviewed Sam and Mary's assets in more detail. First came the assets that passed to Sam automatically because they were owned jointly with right of survivorship:

- The family home
- The chequing and savings accounts
- Two term deposits
- One Canada Savings Bond

Next were the assets that allowed the owner to designate a beneficiary. Mary had designated Sam, so these assets also went to him automatically:

- Mary's RRSP
- Mary's life insurance policy

Finally came the assets in Mary's name only. There were two:

- $5,000 in a savings account that Mary received as a gift from her father a few months before her death
- The motor home, which was registered in Mary's name at the provincial motor vehicle licensing office

The lawyer told Sam that he had good news: probate was not necessary. Sam was surprised, and asked why not. The lawyer explained that transfer of ownership of the first two groups of assets was automatic and never required probate, and that it would be easy and perfectly legal to get the last two assets transferred to Sam without probate.

As for the motor home, the registration papers issued by the provincial government did not amount to legal proof of ownership, the lawyer said. That meant changing registration of the motor home did not require the same degree of formality as changing title to something like a house. All the provincial vehicle licensing office needed was proof of Mary's death and a copy of the unprobated will. Then they would issue a registration card in Sam's name.

The savings account would not likely be a problem either, he said. That's because banks will transfer small accounts to a surviving spouse without a probated will as long as the survivor protects the bank from any claims that might arise. That means giving the bank binding legal assurance that if someone else does have a legal claim to the money the survivor will protect the bank from any liability that might arise. Each bank sets its own limits on the maximum amount of money it will transfer this way, he said, but most of them are comfortable with an amount of $5,000. Sam would have to go to the bank, ask about their limits, and pick up the forms that needed to be signed. He told Sam to bring back the forms before he signed them so the lawyer could look them over and explain them to Sam.

Then the lawyer listed the things that had to be done to officially transfer ownership of the other assets into Sam's name. The items listed by the lawyer are the following:

- Family home: prepare documents to transfer title from Sam and Mary to Sam alone, sign and register the documents in the appropriate land titles office

- Joint bank accounts and savings accounts: take death certificate to the bank and arrange change from Sam and Mary to Sam alone

- Canada Savings Bond: apply to have ownership changed from Sam and Mary jointly to Sam alone

- Mary's RRSP: apply to have funds transferred from Mary's RRSP into Sam's RRSP

- Mary's life insurance: apply to have proceeds paid to Sam as named beneficiary

The lawyer asked Sam if he could handle this himself or if he wanted help. Sam said he could take care of most of it, but he didn't know where to begin as far as the house was concerned. The lawyer said he would be happy to look after that and Sam agreed. He explained that in their province, the land titles office did not accept death certificates from funeral directors as proof of death, so he would have to order an official death certificate from the Vital Statistics Department of the provincial government.

Sam asked if he would need those government death certificates for any of the other institutions he had to deal with, such as the banks and the insurance company. The lawyer said he wasn't sure about each of the banks, but he knew that Sam would need one for the Canada Savings Bond. That's because even though the transfer of the bond was handled through Sam's local bank, the staff there had to send the bond back to the Bank of Canada for processing, and the Bank of Canada did require a provincial death certificate. Sam asked the lawyer to order as many provincial death certificates as Sam needed.

Sam asked the lawyer if there was anything else to worry about. The lawyer said that in other estates the executor had to prepare an inventory, keep careful accounts, advertise for creditors, report to the beneficiaries, and get them to sign releases but none of that applied to Sally's estate. Sam was pleased to hear that, but he wanted to know why not. The lawyer told him it all boiled down to three simple facts. First, Sam was both the executor and the sole beneficiary of Mary. Second, there were no challengers on the horizon. Third, Mary's estate wasreally quite small.

Sam nodded, but asked for more explanation. The lawyer continued, saying that Sam was wearing both hats — Sam was sole beneficiary and sole executor — and Sam already knew what assets Mary owned and what debts she owed. Therefore, there was no need for Sam the executor to create detailed records and accounts that only Sam the beneficiary would ever look at. Also, there was no point in Sam the beneficiary signing a release in favour of Sam the executor.

Next, the lawyer pointed out, hardly any of Mary's assets were coming to Sam as beneficiary of Mary's will. Almost everything was Sam's by joint ownership or by beneficiary designation. By law only the assets that passed through the will were available to creditors or claimants. The jointly owned and designated assets were safe. Besides, the lawyer told Sam, Mary didn't leave any debts except for the items she routinely charged to credit cards, and they were only what were necessary to keep the family in food, clothes, gas, and all the other things of day-to-day life. It was not as if Sam was not going to pay them, and if he didn't, his own credit rating would suffer since those cards were also jointly owned.

Mary's only creditor would be the tax department, but the tax consequences of Mary's death were small, the lawyer said. The jointly owned house was exempt from capital gains tax, her rrsp rolled over into Sam's rrsp tax free, her life insurance proceeds were tax free, the bank accounts, term deposits, and Canada Savings Bond were cash assets that pass tax free, so the only tax owing would be for the income Mary earned on her investments from January 1 to the date of her death. The lawyer told him to go to the cra office and get a T1 return, plus the booklet *Preparing Returns for Deceased Persons*, and wait for Mary's tax reporting slips to come in the mail.

As for challengers to the will, there simply wouldn't be any, the lawyer said. Mary had full mental capacity when she signed it and besides, there was no one else who had a right to claim a share of her estate. Sam thought for a moment and said he had heard something about children having that right. The lawyer agreed, but pointed out that the law makes an exception when the children are minors, are living as a family with the surviving parent, and all the estate goes to that surviving parent. As long as that parent is going to use the assets to continue to look after those kids, they don't have the right to make a claim. Even if the kids did have a right to claim part of Mary's estate, the lawyer added, they could only claim against the assets that go through the will. In Mary's case those assets were so small that a full-scale legal claim wouldn't make sense, he said.

As Sam was preparing to leave the lawyer's office, another question occurred to him. If looking after Mary's estate was going to be so easy, and if the two assets that are in her name can be transferred to Sam without probate of the will, why, Sam wondered, did they bother to do wills in the first place? Good question, the lawyer replied. Because of the wise decisions he and Mary had made about joint ownership, and because Mary had designated Sam as beneficiary of other assets, Sam was right. There was no need for a will, as far as that went.

But, the lawyer asked, what if Mary and Sam had died together in the car crash? Then their wills would be invaluable, he said, because the provisions they made for their children would come into effect. Besides, he said, even though Mary was gone, Sam's will was still valid. If something happened to Sam, now the children were provided for and there was one less detail for Sam to worry about at this difficult time.

Sam thought about it, and about how much time and effort it took Mary to get him into the lawyer's office to do that will, and saw the wisdom of the lawyer's words. He thanked him, and Mary, and left.

In the days that followed Sam picked up the forms that the banks and the insurance company needed. He went back to the lawyer two weeks later. The lawyer had the house documents ready to sign and he explained the bank's indemnity form to Sam (see Sample 3). Sam signed everything, and the lawyer sent the house documents to the land titles office for registration. He gave Sam the extra provincial death certificates and told Sam that he would send Sam the reregistered land title and his bill in a few weeks.

Sam went back to his bank, gave them the death certificates, the Canada Savings Bond, and signed the forms they needed to get the bonds into Sam's name. He sent the application for the insurance money to the insurance company along with a death certificate. He went to the motor vehicles office and got the motor home transferred into his name. He went to Mary's bank, gave them the death certificate and indemnity and got her account transferred into his name.

INDEMNITY

Between *(name of bank)*
And Sam Smith, executor of the estate of Mary Smith, deceased

Whereas Mary Smith died on *(date)* at *(city and province)* leaving a will naming her spouse Sam Smith as executor and sole beneficiary of her estate,

And Sam Smith does not wish to apply for probate because all of Mary Smith's assets pass to him by right of survivorship or by beneficiary designation with the exception of a cash account at *(name of bank),*

Therefore in consideration of the covenants herein the parties agree that:

The bank will transfer the said account to Sam Smith without probate and Sam Smith will fully indemnify the bank and hold it harmless from any and all claims, demands or actions made against it by anyone as a result of the said transfer, including any legal costs the bank might incur defending itself against such claims on a solicitor and his own client basis.

Signed at _____ on _____ .
             (city and Province)   *(date)*

_____
Authorized signing officer of *(name of bank)*

_____
Sam Smith

_____
Witness
(affidavit of execution required)

A few weeks later he received the lawyer's letter containing the amended title to the house and the lawyer's bill. Sam's job as executor was finished and he was pleased at how smoothly everything had gone. What Sam didn't know was that within a year he would find himself acting as executor again. Nor did he know how much more work would be involved in the next estate.

1.1 The eight duties of an executor and the estate of Mary Smith

Sam's position as sole beneficiary and sole executor made his job very simple.

Let's see how what Sam did relates to the eight executor's duties that we discussed in last eight chapters.

1.1a Duty 1: Make reasonable funeral arrangements

As sole beneficiary and sole executor, Sam had full authority to make funeral arrangements without any restrictions. The only constraint was how much he felt he could afford.

1.1b Duty 2: Find and take control of the assets of the deceased

Sam already knew what assets Mary owned in her own name and what assets the two of them owned jointly. He did not have to search for them, and he had control of everything except the bank account in her name. Fortunately, he did not need probate to take control of that account.

1.1c Duty 3: Prepare an inventory, value the assets, and keep an account

You will recall that I listed five reasons in Chapter 5 for keeping an inventory and accounts. Fortunately, none of them applied to Sam. He did not need probate, there were no significant tax consequences of Mary's death, he was the sole beneficiary, and there were no creditors so he did not need the protection these documents offer.

1.1d Duty 4: Find and probate the will, if necessary

Sam found the will easily because he knew exactly where it was — in the lawyer's office.

Probate was not necessary because most assets were jointly owned or were designated to him. The only asset in Mary's name was the bank account, and Sam was able to take control of that by signing an indemnity with the bank.

Also, no one was claiming that Mary's will was invalid — that it was made under pressure or that she did not have mental capacity when she signed it.

1.1e   Duty 5: Deal with debts and other legitimate claims

There were no creditors, nor did anyone have the right to make a claim to part of Mary's estate.

1.1f   Duty 6: Pay any taxes owing by the deceased and the estate

The only tax consequence of Mary's death was to file her T1 terminal return as usual. Sam did not need a clearance certificate because cra was going to get its full due and there was no one else that he had to protect himself from.

1.1g   Duty 7: Account to and get releases from the beneficiaries

Again, as sole beneficiary, Sam did not need to comply with this requirement.

1.1h   Duty 8: Distribute to the beneficiaries

Ownership and control of most of the assets passed to Sam automatically as soon as Mary died. Other than the paperwork necessary to change the records at the appropriate government offices, there was nothing formal that Sam had to do. Also, Sam was able to take ownership of Mary's bank account by signing the bank's indemnity.

2.   Estate 2: Sally Smith — Sam's Mother, an Elderly Widow

A year after Mary died, Sam got another call from the hospital. Could he please come over right away? His mother, Sally, had arrived by ambulance. She'd had a heart attack and it looked serious.

Sally was a widow who lived alone in the same house she and her husband had bought when they got married, back when her husband got out of the army after World War Two. The house was in good shape but much of the maintenance was a struggle for Sally. Sam often suggested she sell it and move to a seniors' centre, but Sally was a feisty, independent woman. She was determined to stay in her home until "they carry me out in a box."

Sally had also become somewhat eccentric in recent years. She was still fully alert and knew exactly what was going on in the world around her — she kept her bills and payments right up to date — but her housekeeping habits had changed. Papers that once would have been neatly placed in a filing cabinet now lay in piles throughout the house. Boxes full of unsorted letters, Christmas cards, and other material filled the basement. Many times Sam had offered to help Sally sort things and clean it up but she always told him to mind his own business. Any discussion about her estate, let alone funeral plans, was totally out of the question.

At the hospital Sam was whisked into an emergency room and was confronted with an array of tubes and machines that he had seen only on television. Sally was lying on a bed underneath it all. The doctor said she'd had a major heart attack and they were doing all they could to help, but it didn't look good. Sam stayed the night, and when the heart monitor stopped beeping the next morning, he held her hand as she drew her last breath.

Once again Sam was overcome with grief, and once again his rational mind tried to help him figure out what to do. He knew Sally had a will, and he thought it appointed him executor, but he'd never seen it. He knew he would have to go through the house as soon as possible to find it. In the meantime, he wanted his mother to have a decent funeral even if he had to pay for it himself. Since he'd had the experience of arranging his wife's funeral a year ago he was ready when the hospital staff asked him which funeral home to call.

Sam met with the funeral director later that afternoon to make arrangements. He mentioned that he didn't have signing authority on his mother's accounts. The funeral director told Sam not to worry. He explained that funeral bills took priority over any other debts of a deceased person, even over income taxes owing, and the banks were very good about releasing funds to pay these bills right out of the deceased's account without any formal paperwork. All Sam needed to do was take the bill to his mother's bank along with a copy of the funeral director's death certificate and they would issue a bank draft payable to the funeral home out of Sally's account.

The funeral director then asked Sam if he wanted to choose a grave marker right away. Sam declined for two reasons. First, Sam knew that grave markers were not considered normal funeral expenses and he needed to know a lot more about his mother's assets before he could decide. Second, Sam had a brother, Nick, who lived in another province. They weren't close — Sam hadn't spoken to him in years — but Sam knew that his mother had kept in touch with Nick. Nick would be in the will, too, and Sam knew he had to find the will as soon as possible. When he left the funeral home he went straight to Sally's house. He wasn't looking forward to what lay ahead.

Sam shuddered as he let himself in Sally's back door. The kitchen was just as he imagined, every surface strewn with paper. How would he ever find the important papers in all this? He feared he would have to go through every piece of paper and that would take time.

Then Sam remembered a filing cabinet in the basement. He went downstairs, opened it, and found a file marked "Will." In the file was a copy of a will done six years earlier by the same lawyer that Sam and Mary had used. As Sam suspected, Sally divided everything equally between Sam and Nick. However, the will said something else that Sam was not expecting. Sally's will appointed Sam and Nick as joint executors. Sam had no idea what he should do now except to call the lawyer. He checked the door locks, plugged a living room light into a timer switch, brought in the day's mail, adjusted the drapes, and went home.

The next day Sam took his copy of the will to the lawyer. Yes, the lawyer had the original in his vault. Yes, Sam and Nick were joint executors. Sam asked what that meant and was told they would have to work together and agree on everything. Sam asked if there was any way to remove his brother as joint executor so Sam could look after things himself. The lawyer said Nick could always renounce the appointment if he wished, but he couldn't be forced to do that. He might be willing to renounce to avoid the hassle of coming back and forth from his home in another province, but that was up to Nick, and they wouldn't know until they asked him.

Sam asked if there was a chance that Sally had done another will after this one — a will that might make Sam sole executor. The lawyer said it was possible that Sally had done another will with another lawyer, but he had no way of knowing that. All he knew was that Sally hadn't come back to him.

Then the lawyer pointed out that none of Sally's assets were owned jointly with either of the boys, nor did she own any designated beneficiary assets like insurance or RRSPs. That meant there would be no shortcuts to getting assets transferred. They would have to get probate of the will. Incidentally, he added, as part of getting probate the executors had to swear that they had not found any other wills. That was another reason to get probate, and a reason to do a very thorough search of Sally's papers.

Sam asked what he should do next. The lawyer told Sam to call his brother, tell him about the death, the funeral arrangements, and the will, and after the funeral he would be happy to meet with the two of them to explain what had to be done. In the meantime, the lawyer told Sam to make sure the house was secure and nothing of value went out the doors. Sam said he had already done that.

Sam went home and made the call. He picked up his brother at the airport the next day. The day after the funeral found them sitting in the lawyer's office together.

The lawyer gave Nick a copy of the will, explained the reasons for a probate application, and asked Nick if he wanted to be joint executor or if Sam could look after the estate alone. Nick asked if he would still be informed if he was not a joint executor, and the lawyer said that Sam was required to prepare a complete inventory of the assets and send a copy to Nick. Also, Sam had to provide Nick with an accounting for everything that went into and out of the estate. Finally, Sam could not pay himself any fees until they were approved by Nick or by a judge of the surrogate court.

Nick said he appreciated the information but he wanted to go through the house with Sam first. Sam said that was fine with him because he could use the help. The lawyer gave them a checklist of things to look for (see Appendix) and they left his office to go to the house.

When they got to Sally's, Nick was surprised by the disarray. They both wondered where to start. Sam suggested starting with the kitchen and working their way through each room on the main floor then on to the basement and garage. Nick agreed and they began. They looked at every piece of paper trying to sort out the wheat from the chaff — the useful and valuable from the garbage.

Sam opened the drawer by the phone, lifted out the phone book, and casually flipped through it. A flurry of brown bank notes fluttered to the floor. Sam picked them up and counted six one hundred dollar bills. At the same moment Nick opened the cutlery drawer and lifted out the plastic cutlery tray. A handful of paper was underneath. He lifted out the pile, put it on the table and fanned out the papers with his hand. In the midst of the old recipes and scraps were three official looking documents. He picked them up. They were mature Canada Savings Bonds worth $5,000 each. The two brothers looked at each other. They realized they were going to have to be very careful because Mom's modest estate might prove to be less modest than they thought.

They kept going through every drawer, cupboard, and closet. They looked under beds and carpets and behind dressers. They checked every pocket of every article of clothing. They found more bank notes and savings bonds. They also found bank statements, bills, and credit card statements. They even found a box containing copies of Sally's tax returns for the last 40 years. When they looked behind the pictures hanging on the walls, they found that each one had a label on the back. Written on each label was a name: Sam or Nick.

In the basement they found stacks of boxes and they went through each one. Finally, in the farthest corner of the garage, they found a box sealed with tape. Sam picked it up and said it was too light for documents. He ripped off the tape and looked inside. He reached in and took out two old baseball gloves.

"Remember these?" he asked Nick.

He passed one to his brother. Nick put it on, smacked the fist of his free hand into the pocket then pressed the glove to his face.

"I loved that smell," he said, "I still do."

The feel and smell of the glove brought back a flood of good memories, and the mistrust that had kept the brothers apart began to slip away.

As they climbed the back porch stairs Nick told Sam that there was no reason for Nick to stay on as joint executor. Nick said he was satisfied that they had found everything of value and that it would only slow things down if Sam and the lawyer had to wait for documents to travel back and forth to Nick for signature. He said he would sign the renunciation as soon as the lawyer could get it ready (see Sample 4). Nick also said that didn't mean Sam would have to do everything himself. Nick said he would be happy to help Sam any way he could.

SAMPLE 4
RENUNCIATION

Surrogate Court of _____
(Province)

Estate of Sally Smith, deceased

Renunciation of Probate

The deceased Sally Smith appointed me joint executor in her will; however, I am unwilling to act in that capacity,

Therefore I hereby renounce all my right and title to a grant of probate in the said will and declare that I have not intermeddled in the said estate.

Signed at _____on _____.
            (city and Province)   *(date)*

_____
Nick Smith

_____
Witness
(affidavit of execution required)

"There's one more thing," said Nick. "Let's pick out a nice headstone for Mom's grave and get it set up. It's the least we can do for her." Sam agreed, thanked him, and the two of them put the cash and bonds into envelopes, locked the door and left.

That evening, Sam filled out the checklist the lawyer had given him. The cash came to $8,000 and the savings bonds to $70,000 face value. They were compounding bonds, which meant the interest was payable only on maturity. Sam had no idea how much interest they had earned. Nor did he know what the house was worth. He guessed $200,000. As for the household goods, Sam had no idea.

The next morning, before Nick's flight home, the two boys found themselves back in the lawyer's office. Sam showed him the completed checklist. Using the information, the lawyer prepared an initial inventory of Sally's assets. For the household goods, he put a nominal value of $1 and told the boys they could insert the true figure once the goods had been sold. (See Sample 5.) Sam said he would find out how much interest was due on the bonds, amend the inventory form and fax a copy to Nick. In fact, he said, he would fax a new version of the inventory to Nick whenever he found a new asset or got new information about the values of the assets they had.

SAMPLE 5
INITIAL INVENTORY FOR ESTATE OF
SALLY SMITH, DECEASED

Initial Inventory for Estate of Sally Smith, Deceased

Land:

Personal residence at *(insert address)*; approximate value	$200,000

Cash:

Found in residence	$8,000
In bank account at *(insert name of branch)*; exact amount to be determined	$1

Canada Savings Bonds: *(insert serial numbers and series number)*

Face value only	$70,000

Household Goods:

Nominal value only	$1
TOTAL ASSETS	**$278,002**

Nick agreed that he and Sam would take the pictures that Sally had labelled for them, and since neither of them needed any of the household goods, Sam could send whatever he chose to charity and arrange a garage sale for the rest. Anything that didn't sell he could throw out.

The lawyer confirmed that anyone can deposit money into an existing account, even after that person is dead, so it was okay for Sam to deposit the cash they found into Sally's existing account. He also told them they didn't need to wait for probate to pay the funeral bill. The bank would issue a draft payable to the funeral home right out of Sally's account. All Sam had to do was take the bill to her bank branch. To keep the utilities going until the house was sold, all Sam had to do was call the various companies and tell them that Sally had died and that Sam was in the process of getting probate of her will. He would pay them as soon as he got formal control of her account.

Sam said he knew some good realtors and he would call three of them for an evaluation of the house. Nick asked if those reports could be faxed to him too, then Sam could choose one of them to handle the sale. The lawyer reminded Sam that he couldn't close a sale until probate was issued but he could sign a listing agreement right away so the realtor could start looking for buyers. Sam said he would do that as soon as he had the place emptied out and cleaned up. Nick said it would be okay with him if Sam wanted to hire people to do the cleaning.

The two boys agreed that the lawyer would make the probate application, and he asked them if they wanted to advertise for creditors. They debated that for a few minutes. On the one hand, they had looked at every piece of paper that had come in Sally's door for the last ten years and they felt they had a pretty good handle on to whom she owed money. Outside of the credit cards and house and personal expenses, there weren't any surprises. On the other hand, if they were wrong, and there was a big unknown debt, now was the time to find that out. They agreed to advertise, and the lawyer said he would look after it.

The lawyer reminded them that Sally's estate was entitled to a death benefit from the Canada Pension Plan, and Sam said he would call about that.

The lawyer asked about Sally's taxes. The boys told him they had found a file with tax returns in it, and that Sally was current to the end of the previous year. Sam said he would ask his accountant to look over the most recent years' returns and tell him what had to be done to get a clearance certificate for Sally's estate.

Finally, the lawyer asked about executor's fees. Nick said that he could see this was going to be a lot of work and it would take quite a bit of Sam's time. Nick insisted that Sam keep track of the hours he was going to put in and charge the estate a reasonable fee for this work. He asked the lawyer what that would be, and the lawyer said when a family member acted as executor, the fees often came to 4 percent or 5 percent of the value of the estate.

However, the lawyer went on, before Sam could pay himself anything, he had to send Nick a statement showing what he was asking for and how it was calculated. He said that was usually done at the end just before the executor is ready to hand over funds to the beneficiaries. If the beneficiaries didn't agree with the figure then the executor had to apply to a judge for approval of his fee and his handling of the estate assets. The judge would look at the size and complexity of the estate, the amount of work done and the level of expertise required and set a fee accordingly. Nick said he was sure that wouldn't be necessary and he looked forward to hearing more from Sam as things went along.

They agreed that the lawyer would handle the probate application and then arrange to transfer the house into the estate so Sam could sell it. The lawyer said he would need values for each of the assets and Sam said he would track down that information. Then they left the lawyer's office and Sam drove Nick to the airport.

In the days that followed, Sam cleaned out the house. He took the pictures that had his name on the back and sent Nick's to him. Then he gave some useful items to charity and held a garage sale for the rest. The sale brought in $2,000. Anything that didn't sell he threw away.

Then he contacted three real estate agents. They agreed to give him written evaluations of the home based on recent sales of similar properties in the area. The evaluations ranged from a high of $270,000 to a low of $250,000. Sam faxed these to Nick and recommended they list at the high figure and be prepared to accept the low one. Nick agreed, so Sam selected a realtor and signed a listing agreement. Sam reminded the realtor that any potential buyers had to understand that Sam couldn't transfer title until he had probate so any offers had to allow a reasonable time for that to happen.

Sam went to the bank, told them of his mother's death and said he needed to know how much cash was in her account and how much the Canada Savings Bonds were worth for purposes of probate. He also said he had found cash in her house and he wanted to deposit it into her account. The bank made the deposit and told him the account balance. Sam was surprised to learn that she now had $35,000 in that account. The bank also looked up the matured value of the bonds. They came to $130,000. The bank said they couldn't cash the bonds until Sam had probate.

Finally, Sam contacted the Canada Pension office and was told his mother's benefit would be approximately $1,800 but they couldn't process the application without probate.

Sam gave all these figures to the lawyer and faxed an updated inventory to Nick. The lawyer then got busy with the probate application. First, he placed an ad in the newspaper calling on any creditors of Sally's estate to bring in proof of their claims within the allotted time. Then he sent Nick a formal renunciation of his appointment as joint executor. Nick signed it and returned it, and when no claims came in from creditors, the lawyer called Sam to come in and sign the papers. Then he sent them to the surrogate court for processing.

The realtor had no trouble getting a good offer on the house, because even though it was small, it was in a desirable neighbourhood where young couples were spending lots of money on additions. Sam was happy to accept a deal at $263,000, subject to obtaining probate within three months.

A probate certificate confirming Sam's appointment as executor came from the court house within six weeks, and the house sale closed. As part of closing, Sam paid off all the utility bills, and the accounts were transferred to the new owners. The price of the house was lowered by the amount of Sally's portion of the annual property tax so that the buyers would pay the whole amount when the bills came out from the city. Then Sam paid off the outstanding balances on his mother's credit cards.

Sam took the certified copy of the probate certificate to the bank. They cashed the bonds and deposited the money into his mother's account. Then they changed the account to "The Estate of Sally Smith, Sam Smith Executor" and confirmed Sam's signing authority on it.

Sam took another certified copy of the probate certificate to the Canada Pension office and they processed the death benefit application. The cheque came payable to Sam as executor, and he deposited it into the estate account.

Armed with the tax returns and the values shown in the probate application, Sam went to his accountant. He was pleased to hear that Sally's tax situation was not complicated. The accountant told Sam that Sally had declared the interest from the Canada Savings Bonds every year so she was liable only for this year's interest. As well, since her only other income was her Old Age Security and her small Canada Pension payment, her tax liability would not be much higher than the $5,000 she had paid the year before.

The accountant said he would file the return now but there was no need for Sam to wait several months for a clearance certificate before releasing money to himself and his brother. Instead Sam could holdback $10,000 for taxes and accounting fees and split the rest with his brother now. Then, when the clearance certificate came, Sam would have enough to pay the taxes owing. If the tax assessment was higher than expected, Sam had extra in hand. If that extra was not needed, he could split it with his brother then.

Sam began to prepare a statement for his brother. First, though, he had to decide how much he was going to claim for his work as executor. Sam looked at the notes he had kept of the time he put in. The notes showed a total of about 40 hours, though Sam knew he hadn't kept track of everything. He decided to ask for $2,000 for his trouble, and the lawyer said that was very reasonable. Sam prepared a final inventory (see Sample 6) and an accounting that showed the money received by the estate, the expenses paid, the $2,000 executor's fee, the $10,000 tax holdback, and the balance to be divided in half between them (see Sample 7). He sent them to Nick for signing and approval, and they came back by return mail, so he sent Nick a cheque.

Two months later he received an assessment from cra confirming the tax calculated by the accountant and a clearance certificate. Sam then sent Nick a cheque for half the remainder, closed Sally's account, and realized his job as executor was over. Sam was relieved. He'd never imagined he would ever have to be an executor, certainly not twice in one year, and he hoped he would never have to do it again.

FINAL INVENTORY, ESTATE OF SALLY SMITH, DECEASED

Land: Residence *(insert address)*

Sale price	$263,000
Less closing costs *(give details)*	$3,000
Net value	$260,000

Cash: *(insert name and address of bank branch and account number)*

Balance at death	$27,000
+ Deposits (give details)	$8,000
– Withdrawals (give details)	$2,000
Balance on hand	$33,000

Canada Savings Bonds: *(give serial numbers and series of bonds)*

Total face value	$70,000
+ Interest received	$60,000
Total value	$130,000
Canada Pension Plan Death Benefit:	$1,800
Household Goods: proceeds of garage sale	$2,000
Total Assets:	$426,800

Debts:		
	Funeral *(give details)*	$12,000
	Gravestone	$2,000
	Credit Cards	
	(give details of accounts and amounts)	$1,500
Total Debts:		$15,500

Total Assets	$426,800
– Total Debts	$15,500
= Total on Hand:	**$411,300**

ACCOUNT FOR DISTRIBUTION PURPOSES, ESTATE OF SALLY SMITH, DECEASED

Account For Distribution Purposes
Estate of Sally Smith, Deceased

Assets on hand per Inventory	$411,300
Less	
Holdback pending Clearance Certificate from CRA	$10,000
Estimated Legal Fees *(identify law firm)*	$1,500
Estimated accounting fees *(identify firm)*	$1,500
Proposed executor's fee	$2,000
Probate fee *(will vary from province to province)*	$1,500
Amount available for distribution	$394,800
Proposed distribution:	
½ to Sam Smith	$197,400
½ to Nick Smith	$197,400

Approved:

_____

Nick Smith

2.1 The eight duties of an executor and the estate of Sally Smith

Sam's job was more complicated this time for a variety of reasons. First, he did not have any advance knowledge about his mother's assets and affairs nor about the terms of her will. Second, he was not the sole executor, and third, he was not the sole beneficiary. As a result, he had to follow procedures and comply with each of the eight executor's duties.

2.1a Duty 1: Make reasonable funeral arrangements

Sally did not leave Sam any hints about her funeral. She did not prearrange anything nor did she tell Sam what she wanted. Also, Sam had no idea what her estate could afford. All he could do was guess, in the conviction that he would cover the bill if he had to. Having recently been through his wife's funeral, Sam was familiar with costs and procedures and was able to use that knowledge to make reasonable arrangements. He also knew that headstones were not included in funeral expenses so he held off on that until he had a chance to consult with his brother. As it turned out, the estate was able to cover everything and his brother was in favour of a suitable headstone.

2.1b Duty 2: Find and take control of the assets of the deceased

Sam's first job was to do a quick inspection of Sally's home, deal with perishable items, and then make sure the place was secure while he awaited the arrival of his brother and confirmation of his status as executor. That was wise because it turned out that he and his brother were joint executors, which gave his brother an equal say as well as an equal share of the responsibilities.

Because his brother was also a beneficiary, and because none of Sally's assets were joint with the boys nor were any assets designated to them, Sam and Nick had to wait until probate was issued before they could take formal control. In the meantime, they could go through the house and dispose of items they did not want or that did not have any resale value.

2.1c Duty 3: Prepare an inventory, value the assets, and keep an account

Sam began to fill out the checklist the lawyer gave him as soon as he got it, and this served as the estate inventory. He updated it as new information was available. This information was necessary for all the reasons that I mentioned in Chapter 5 — for the probate application, for the tax accountant, for his brother the other beneficiary, for any creditors, and ultimately for his own protection.

2.1d Duty 4: Find and probate the will if necessary

Sam had to search for the will, but fortunately his mother had a copy in her filing cabinet which led Sam back to the lawyer who held the original in his vault. Probate was necessary because none of Sally's assets passed by right of survivorship and none were designated to the boys. Also, they needed to be sure this was in fact the last will, that there were no unpaid creditors, that no one was challenging the will on grounds of undue pressure or lack of mental capacity, and to confirm the authority of the executors in the eyes of the outside world.

After searching the house with Sam for assets, Nick decided that he was comfortable renouncing his position as joint executor and he signed the necessary paper so that Sam could be appointed as sole executor of the estate.

2.1e Duty 5: Deal with debts and other claimants against the estate

Expenses that came with owning and operating a house, such as municipal taxes, heat, light, water, and telephone, were expected and would get paid when the house sold. Other debts were a problem because neither son was familiar with Sally's affairs. Therefore, it was necessary to advertise for creditors in order to establish a cut off date for claims, which also protects the executor.

Getting probate also sets a deadline for any claims that might be made by others who think they have a claim to a share of the assets and to those who think that the will was signed under pressure or when Sally was without mental capacity.

2.1f Duty 6: Pay any taxes owing by the deceased and the estate

The only tax consequence of Sally's death was filing the T1 terminal return, but since Sam and Nick were not familiar with Sally's affairs, they decided to hire an accountant to file it for them. He pointed out that they did need a clearance certificate.

2.1g Duty 7: Account to and get releases from the beneficiaries

Sam did prepare an accounting, which he sent to Nick for approval along with a formal release (see Sample 8), so his brother would have complete information about the estate. He also did it because he was making a claim for an executor's fee and the accounting is the place to disclose that. As it turned out, Nick was satisfied with the amounts, signed the forms and returned them to Sam.

2.1h Duty 8: Distribute to the beneficiaries

Assets were distributed in two stages, on the advice of the accountant. The first distribution occurred after the accountant calculated the tax owing and advised Sam to hold back twice as much in case the cra challenged the figure or in case any unexpected debts came up. After the tax return was accepted, and cra issued a clearance certificate, Sam released the hold back.

SAMPLE 8
RELEASE

Surrogate Court of _____
                         (Province)

Estate of Sally Smith, Deceased

Release

I, Nick Smith, of _____ acknowledge that I have received
                    (City and Province)
from Sam Smith, Executor of the estate of Sally Smith, Deceased, a full and satisfactory accounting for and full payment of all amounts owing to me from the said estate,

Therefore I release Sam Smith and his successors from any and all liability arising out of his management of the said estate.

Signed at _____on _____.
          (city and Province)   *(date)*

_____
Nick Smith

In the presence of

_____
Witness *(affidavit of execution required)*

APPENDIX

CHECKLIST: THE EIGHT DUTIES OF AN EXECUTOR

Duty 1: Make reasonable funeral arrangements

- ❏ Determine if deceased arranged prepaid funeral plan
- ❏ If not, make funeral arrangements in line with size of deceased's estate
- ❏ If deceased left funeral instructions, follow those if reasonable
- ❏ Do not purchase grave marker without prior consent of beneficiaries

Duty 2: Find and take control of assets of deceased

- ❏ Secure deceased's residence and contents
  - ❏ Remove and dispose of perishables
  - ❏ Secure portable valuables and remove if necessary
  - ❏ Secure collections and collectibles
  - ❏ Arrange ongoing payment of household utilities if necessary
- ❏ Search for important papers
  - ❏ Tax returns
  - ❏ Bank statements
  - ❏ Material from other financial institutions
  - ❏ Insurance policies

- ❏ Business records
- ❏ Stocks, bonds, and share certificates
- ❏ Cash
- ❏ Will
- ❏ Evidence of loans owing to deceased by others
- ❏ Cancel
  - ❏ Credit cards
  - ❏ Newspaper
  - ❏ Magazine subscriptions
- ❏ Reroute mail
- ❏ Secure vehicles
- ❏ Confirm insurance coverage
  - ❏ Residence and contents
  - ❏ Vehicles
- ❏ Contact employer of deceased
  - ❏ Check on pension benefits
  - ❏ Arrange receipt of final paycheque
  - ❏ Make any available insurance claims
  - ❏ Contact CPP re: death benefit

Duty 3: Prepare an inventory, value the assets, and keep an account
- ❏ Complete inventory of estate assets
- ❏ Establish estate bank account
- ❏ Open new estate account
- ❏ Use existing account of deceased
- ❏ Take pictures of assets
- ❏ Arrange evaluations
  - ❏ Real estate
    - ❏ Realtor's market valuation
    - ❏ Appraisal by licensed appraiser
  - ❏ Vehicles
    - ❏ Car dealer valuation

- ❏ Comparable vehicles in newspaper
- ❏ Household goods
    - ❏ Personal property appraiser
    - ❏ Executor's best estimate
    - ❏ Nominal value only

Duty 4: Find and probate the will, if necessary

- ❏ Finding the will
    - ❏ Search the residence
    - ❏ Contact the deceased's lawyer
    - ❏ Look in safety deposit box
    - ❏ Confirm beneficiaries
    - ❏ Obtain addresses and contact information
- ❏ Probating the will
    - ❏ Is probate necessary?
    - ❏ Joint with right of survivorship assets go to the joint owner automatically
    - ❏ Designated assets go to designated beneficiary
    - ❏ Cash only accounts may transfer on indemnity and release basis
    - ❏ Other solely owned assets require probate
    - ❏ Other reasons for probate
        - ❏ To eliminate creditors through advertising
        - ❏ To identify or eliminate claims by spouse or dependants through serving notice on potential claimants
        - ❏ To eliminate challenges to validity of the will itself
        - ❏ To confirm status as executor and eliminate challengers

Duty 5: Deal with debts and other claims

- ❏ Debts relating to the death
  Bank will issue draft payable to funeral home

- ❏ Establish debts of deceased
  - ❏ Business or partnership debts
  - ❏ Medical bills
  - ❏ Claims by caregivers
  - ❏ Ongoing child or spousal support
  - ❏ Leases, mortgages
  - ❏ Lawsuits against deceased
  - ❏ Credit card bills
  - ❏ Loans owing by deceased
- ❏ Advertise for creditors
- ❏ Review proof of claims
- ❏ Pay valid claims
- ❏ Notify potential spouse, dependants, and other potential claimants
- ❏ Respond to any legal documents they file
- ❏ Defend legal action as required

Duty 6: Pay any taxes owing by the deceased and the estate

- ❏ Obtain and review previous year's returns
- ❏ File previous year's returns if necessary
- ❏ File T1 Terminal return for deceased
- ❏ File rights and things returns and other optional returns if necessary
- ❏ File T3 for estate if necessary
- ❏ Request clearance certificate
- ❏ Review GST status of deceased

Duty 7: Account to and get releases from beneficiaries

- ❏ Establish executor's fee
- ❏ Prepare final account and releases and send to the beneficiaries

Duty 8: Distribute to the beneficiaries

- ❏ Obtain signed releases and approval of accounts
- ❏ Holdback sufficient funds for tax and other liabilities pending clearance certificate
- ❏ Obtain clearance certificate
- ❏ Release balance of funds to beneficiaries

GLOSSARY

Administrator

> a person, appointed by the surrogate court, to look after the estate of someone who died without a will

Advertising for creditors

> placing ads in the local newspaper to notify creditors of the deceased of the time limit for providing proof of their claims to the executor

Alternate executor

> a person named in a will as a backup executor in case the named executor cannot act

Beneficiary

> a person named in a will to receive a gift or benefit from the estate of the testator after the testator dies

CRA

> Canada Revenue Agency, formerly known as Canada Customs and Revenue Agency

Capital asset

> an asset that attracts capital gain tax according to the rules set by the federal government from time to time

Capital gain

> the increased value of an asset being the difference between its cost price and its fair market value at a later date such as date of death

Capital gain inclusion rate

> the percentage of the capital gain set by the federal government from time to time that is included in taxable income

Capital gain tax

> the tax imposed by the federal government on capital gains

Clearance certificate

a letter from CRA confirming that all taxes owing by the deceased and the estate are paid

Conversion

selling an asset for cash

Cost price

the original value of a capital asset

Creditors

those to whom the deceased owed money

Deemed disposition

a pretend sale for capital gain purposes triggered by certain events such as death

Designated beneficiary asset

a type of asset that is allowed by law to pass directly to a named beneficiary at death without probate, such as life insurance and RRSPs

Devastavit

loss of or damage to estate assets

Estate

all the assets and valuables owned by a person at death

Estate account

an account kept by an executor of all money received by and paid out of an estate

Estate inventory

a record kept by an executor of all assets in an estate and their values

Executor

the person named in a will to handle the estate of the testator at death

Holdback

money kept by the executor until CRA issues a clearance certificate

Holograph will

a will entirely in the handwriting of the deceased

Indemnity

a promise to reimburse someone if he or she incurs a loss because he or she gave something to you or did something for you

Insolvent estate

an estate that does not have enough assets to pay its creditors

In specie

keeping an asset as it is for delivery to a beneficiary, as opposed to converting it (selling it for cash)

Intermeddling

doing something that gives others the impression that you are executor of an estate when you are not

Joint executor

a person named in a will to act as executor along with someone else

Joint tenancy

joint ownership with right of survivorship

Per capita

each member of the group gets an equal share

Per stirpes

each member of the group gets the same share as other members of his or her generation

Personal representative

a term meaning both executor and administrator of an estate

Precatory memorandum

a list made by a testator separate from the will telling the executor to whom the testator would like the listed items to go after death

Probate

the process of proving that a will is the true last will of the deceased

Probate certificate

a certificate issued by the surrogate court confirming that a will is the true last will of a deceased

Probate court

the court that handles probate applications

Renunciation

giving up the right to act as executor

Right of survivorship

the right of a joint owner of an asset to receive that asset automatically on the death of the other joint owner

Rights and things

amounts that a deceased was entitled to but had not yet received at death

Rollover

passing of assets to a beneficiary free of capital gain tax

RRIF

Registered Retirement Income Fund

RRSP

Registered Retirement Savings Plan

Serving notice

notifying potential beneficiaries or claimants of their right to make a claim either by delivering documents to them or by publishing a notice in a newspaper

Sole executor

an executor named in a will to act alone

Spousal trust

a trust that gives all the benefits to the spouse of the person setting it up

Surrogate court

the court that handles estate and probate matters

Tainted spousal trust

a spousal trust that also benefits someone other than the spouse

Tax deferral

delaying payment of tax until a future date or event according to rules set by the federal government

Tenancy in common

joint ownership that does not include the right of survivorship

Terminal return

the T1 return that is required when a person dies

Testator

a person who makes a will

Transfer agent

a company that records transfers of corporate shares after they are sold on the open market

Vacancy rider

a clause in a house insurance policy that extends coverage even though the house is vacant

Waste

loss or damage to estate assets